Solving Equations
An Algebra Intervention

Bradley S. Witzel

Winthrop University

Paul J. Riccomini

The Pennsylvania State University

Boston   Columbus   Indianapolis   New York   San Francisco   Upper Saddle River
Amsterdam   Cape Town   Dubai   London   Madrid   Milan   Munich   Paris   Montreal   Toronto
Delhi   Mexico City   Sao Paulo   Sydney   Hong Kong   Seoul   Singapore   Taipei   Tokyo

Vice President and Editor in Chief: Jeffery W. Johnston
Executive Editor: Ann Castel Davis
Editorial Assistant: Penny Burleson
Senior Managing Editor: Pamela D. Bennett
Senior Project Manager: Sheryl Glicker Langner
Senior Operations Supervisor: Matthew Ottenweller
Senior Art Director: Diane C. Lorenzo

Cover Designer: Candace Rowley
Cover Art: OJO Image/Superstock
Full-Service Project Management: Kelly Ricci, Aptara®, Inc.
Composition: Aptara®, Inc.
Printer/Binder: Bind-Rite Graphics
Cover Printer: Lehigh-Phoenix
Text Font: Sabon

Credits and acknowledgments borrowed from other sources and reproduced, with permission, in this textbook appear on appropriate page within text.

Every effort has been made to provide accurate and current Internet information in this book. However, the Internet and information posted on it are constantly changing, so it is inevitable that some of the Internet addresses listed in this textbook will change.

Library of Congress Cataloging-in-Publication Data
Witzel, Bradley S.
    Solving equations: an algebra intervention/Bradley S. Witzel, Paul J. Riccomini.
        p. cm.
    ISBN-13: 978-0-205-56740-9
    ISBN-10: 0-205-56740-1
    1. Algebra—Study and teaching (Middle school)—United States.   2. Algebra—Study and teaching (Secondary school)—United States.   3. Students with disabilities—Education—United States.
I.   Riccomini, Paul J. II. Title.
    QA159.W58 2010
    512.0071'2—dc22
                                                    2010013332

10 9 8 7 6 5 4 3 2 1

www.pearsonhighered.com

ISBN 10:   0-205-56740-1
ISBN 13: 978-0-205-56740-9

About the Authors

Dr. Bradley Witzel is an associate professor, assistant department chair of multiple academic programs, and director of the special education programs at Winthrop University in Rock Hill, South Carolina. He has experience in the classroom as an inclusive and self-contained teacher of students with high-incidence disabilities and as a classroom assistant and classroom teacher of students with low-incidence disabilities. He has written numerous research practitioner articles on mathematics and motivational instruction for students with and without disabilities. In addition, he frequently provides professional presentations on mathematics-related topics. Dr. Witzel holds a B.S. in psychology and special education from James Madison University and M.Ed. and Ph.D. degrees in special education from the University of Florida.

Dr. Paul J. Riccomini is an associate professor in the Department of Educational and School Pyschology and Special Education at The Pennsylvania State University. He taught mathematics for several years to students in Grades 7–12 with high-incidence disabilities. He has also taught general education math classes to high school students. Dr. Riccomini conducts numerous professional development workshops focusing on improving the mathematics instructional programs for students struggling in math, low-achieving students, and students with learning disabilities through the application of evidenced-based instructional practices. Dr. Riccomini holds a B.A. in mathematics and an M.Ed. in special education from Edinboro University of Pennsylvania. He received his doctorate in special education from the Pennsylvania State University.

Much appreciation goes to Ms. Jaylene Fritz-Patterson for her professionalism and precision as she developed select artwork included in this manual. Currently a high school student, she shows great promise toward her career.

Contents

Introduction

This manual contains the information you will need to implement *Solving Equations: An Algebra Intervention* for students who have yet to fully master solving for unknowns. In the first section, we present a rationale for the importance of providing effective instruction in algebra to *all* students, including students with disabilities. In the overview section, we explain the three basic stages in the Concrete to Representational to Abstract (CRA) instructional sequence and why CRA should be used to build conceptual and procedural knowledge with simple equations. Although this intervention is designed for students in Grades 6–8, it is applicable to students of any age who have not completely learned solving equations. The next section includes a list and description of all manipulatives necessary for the implementation of this intervention. In the final section, we provide an overview of the lesson scripts to be used as guides during teacher-directed lessons. (All of the teacher-directed lessons are presented in the form of scripts.) These scripts were designed as guides to help you use this intervention. We strongly encourage you to become familiar with scripts *prior* to presenting lessons to your students. Please note that this intervention is intended for students who have already received instruction in the area of missing addends and have struggled; therefore, a well-prepared teacher is essential to maximize the effectiveness of this intervention. Students should already be proficient in computation of whole numbers and fractions.

WHY ALGEBRA?

Success in high school algebra is becoming increasingly important to today's students. Algebra is considered by many to serve as gatekeeper to postsecondary education (National Mathematics Advisory Panel [NMAP], 2008). Successful completion of algebra is also essential to a wide variety of employment opportunities (NMAP, 2008). For those who master basic algebraic concepts, it opens doors to more advanced mathematical topics. Algebra closes doors to postsecondary education and technology-based careers for those who do not master it. In addition, many states now require ALL students to pass algebra competency exams or algebra classes to obtain a standard high school diploma.

Given the emphasis placed on algebra, the performance level of both students with disabilities (e.g., learning disabilities, behavior disorders) and their low-achieving nondisabled peers is a serious concern. Students with disabilities experience difficulties learning math; their problems surface early and continue throughout their education (Sanders, Riccomini, & Witzel, 2005; Witzel, Mercer, & Miller, 2003). Moreover, higher-order thinking skills, such as problem solving, are major hurdles for students with disabilities (Cawley & Miller, 1989; Hutchinson, 1993), resulting in many having difficulty in high-school math courses (Miles & Forcht, 1995).

Students with disabilities are not the only ones who struggle with algebra, however. In the 2000 National Assessment of Educational Progress (NAEP), only 2% of U.S. students attained advanced levels of mathematics achievement by Grade 12. Further, large numbers of U.S. students continue to score below the basic level in mathematics. In the 2003 NAEP, 23% of Grade 4 students and 32% of Grade 8 students scored below the "basic" level. Poor algebra performance also is observed in students enrolled in college-level coursework (Kieran, 1992). Concern also exists about gender discrepancies, with females being underrepresented in upper mathematics courses. Those most seriously affected by lack of algebraic skills, however, are often students from minority groups (Lacampagne, 1995). Clearly, many types of struggling students—young women, minorities, students with disabilities, and students from lower socioeconomic households—struggle with success in upper-level mathematics courses.

A need also exists to develop more efficient and effective algebra interventions for both struggling nondisabled students and students with disabilities; but only a small number of empirically based reports on mathematics interventions address algebraic concepts and skills for struggling students (Maccini, McNaughton, & Ruhl, 1999; NMAP, 2008; Riccomini & Witzel, 2010; Witzel, Mercer, & Miller, 2003). *Solving Equations: An Algebra Intervention* provides teachers an evidenced-based intervention (Witzel et al., 2003) focused on helping students better understand five initial areas of equations: (1) simplifying expressions, (2) one-step inverse operations, (3) two+-step inverse operations, (4) simplifying and solving equations, and (5) transformational equations.

Students in algebra often struggle with precursor mathematics skills such as computation with whole numbers, computation with positive and negative integers, and all areas involving fractions (NMAP, 2008). But they also struggle with solving for unknowns in simple equations. Within algebra, students must accurately and fluently solve for unknowns when working with equations in various problem schemata. This program will help build conceptual understanding of solving for unknowns as well as focusing on building fluency with the procedures required to solve simple equations. Students completing this program will be better prepared to work with more concept algebra equations.

 ## OVERVIEW

Proficiency in mathematics depends on a continuous development and blending of intricate combinations of various critical component skills. Gaps in any of these component skills will cause students to struggle in many aspects of their mathematics education. This is especially true for students with math disabilities (MD). The challenges that students with MD encounter during their mathematics instruction are substantial and well documented (see Maccini, Mulcahy, & Wilson, 2007; NMAP, 2008; Riccomini & Witzel, 2010; Sanders et al., 2005). The deficits in mathematics for students with MD are documented in the areas of basic facts, computation procedures, fractions, and solving word problems. Since many of these deficit areas are prerequisite skills for algebra, it prefigures that these students will struggle with algebraic concepts.

Recently, the struggles of students with MD have received a great deal of attention by educators and researchers with renewed emphasis on providing evidenced-based instruction. The NMAP (2008), in an attempt to improve the math instruction in the United States, has provided over 50 suggestions. The panel specifically addressed the instructional needs of low-achieving students and students with disabilities by stating that explicit and systematic instruction is consistently demonstrated in the research as having positive student outcomes in the area of mathematics (NMAP, 2008). The panel went on to assert that students who are struggling should have regular access to explicit and systematic methods of instruction that include clear models with think-alouds, many examples and opportunities for practice, and frequent feedback. This intervention is designed around those recommendations and based on one especially effective instructional approach: Concrete to Representation to Abstract (CRA) instructional sequence.

Teaching students through three levels of learning from concrete objects to matching pictorial representations then finally to abstract numerals is called the CRA sequence of instruction. As its name implies, the CRA instructional sequence systematically and explicitly instructs students through three levels of learning: (1) concrete, (2) representational, and (3) abstract. The purposeful transition through each of the three stages encourages students to learn concepts as well as the procedures and computations so important in mathematics. CRA is a three-level learning process in which students problem solve mathematics through the physical manipulation of concrete materials followed by learning through pictorial representations of the concrete manipulations and ending with solving mathematics through abstract notation (Witzel, 2005). Other terms that have been used to describe this sequence of instruction have been the *concrete to semiconcrete to abstract* sequence of instruction and *graduated* instruction (Gagnon & Maccini, 2007).

Teaching students through the three learning stages in CRA has been shown to be beneficial to secondary students with math difficulties (Butler, Miller, Crehan, Babbitt, & Pierce, 2003; Hutchinson, 1993; Jordan, Miller, & Mercer, 1999; Maccini & Hughes, 2000; NMAP, 2008; Witzel & Riccomini, 2009; Witzel et al., 2003). Success using this sequence of instruction has been beneficial from small group settings to whole-class instruction for students with and without learning difficulties (Witzel, 2005). While other CRA approaches may exist, this one has a history of powerful effects. With the CRA stepwise approach implemented within this instructional series, students with learning disabilities performed at 2 to 3 times the success rates of their traditionally taught peers (Witzel et al., 2003). Moreover, students with a history of performing at or above grade level scored significantly higher than their traditionally taught peers when taught using this approach (Witzel, 2005).

There are many reasons why CRA has been so successful. For one, multimodal interactions with concrete materials and pictorial representations increase the likelihood that students will remember stepwise procedural options in math problem solving. Students are more likely to memorize, encode, and retrieve information when information is presented in a multisensory format: visually, auditorily, tactilely, and kinesthetically. Using the concrete objects and linked pictorial representations described in this program, students will gain access to difficult abstract instructional ideas. What's more, even when students are presented abstract questions in mathematics, they may turn to previous levels of learning, pictorial or concrete, to solve the problem. Thus, the student can solve difficult abstract problems without thinking fluently at the abstract level.

Solving Equations: An Algebra Intervention is designed to help improve mathematics instruction for students who have not fully mastered solving for unknowns at both the conceptual and procedural levels. Although many have advocated for the use of the CRA instructional sequence, very few programs are available for teachers. *Solving Equations: An Algebra Intervention* has been developed to help guide teachers' instructional planning for students with MD in solving simple equations and is supported in the work of Witzel et al. (2003) and Witzel (2005).

DESCRIPTION OF MANIPULATIVES

Inherent in the CRA approach are the hands-on interactions by teachers and students with the concrete objects or manipulatives. For CRA to be effective, there is no one set of appropriate manipulatives. Instead, students should all have access to a set of manipulatives that show the process of solving the problem. The many benefits of a CRA instructional approach (e.g., improved math outcomes, deeper processing of math concepts) will only be realized when each student has the opportunity to interact in a purposeful and engaging series of activities. Manipulatives take many different forms and are available for purchase through education supply companies or can simply be made using materials found at a local superstore. What is important is that the materials must be available to both teachers and students.

Since there is no one set of absolute materials that must be purchased, we suggest a set of materials that go with instructional intervention. The following manipulative objects coordinate with the concrete lessons within this intervention, and templates can be found in the appendix. However, you will need to acquire popsicle sticks, a string for an equal sign, and condiment or bathroom cups for groups. Some teachers substitute commercial materials for these household items, but most appreciate the disposable and easily replaceable items listed here.

- 20 digit sticks
- 4 tens sticks
- 12 group cups
- 4 multiplication symbols
- 1 equal sign
- 8 minus signs
- 8 plus signs

DIGITS

Digits are the mathematical notation most often manipulated. It is important to use materials that are easily moved and can be picked up with the least deft fingers in class. Also, since so many digits must be used in representing the integers, it is important to have ones that are easy to obtain and replace. We recommend short popsicle sticks. as they are easy to pick up, readily available, and easy to see on a tabletop.

How to use: When students are learning through the concrete phase, you may refer to sticks as sticks. However, teach them that the collection of sticks is considered a total number. For example, when looking at 5 sticks, refer to the set as "5 sticks." When the students are being taught a representational lesson, refer to the set as "5 tallies" or tick marks. Always include the abstract verbal marker of 5, though, because when they are being taught in the important abstract lessons, you want to refer to the sticks only as 5.

TENS

While tens are not as frequently used in the concrete stage of this instructional set, their place is important. You may find yourself helping students connect larger abstractly  written numbers to this concrete set of materials. Just as with base-ten blocks, the tens should look significantly larger than the digits, as they physically represent a larger place value. We recommend using tongue depressors to outweigh the small popsicle sticks.

How to use: Use the ten sticks similarly to how you use the digit sticks. For example, with a representation of 20, say "2 ten sticks" during concrete lessons. During the representational level, say "1 ten" for each darker straight line drawn.

GROUP

Students with memory problems are often asked to memorize basic facts. When they fail to do so, there are many means for memorization. However, there are few attempts at explaining how we compute numbers and why the answers are what they are. For multiplication and division, using a physical representation for grouping is important.

Using this representation allows for more explanation about what is occurring during the computation rather than requesting students to memorize basic facts that have not yet been mastered. For example, 4×6 and 6×4 are not the same computational problem. While their answers are the same, the purpose of each number is different. In the example, 4×6 means there are 4 groups of 6 objects each. Since multiplication involves totals, we look at the number of objects as the answer—24 in this case. Using the commutative property, these assignments can be reversed to achieve the same number, but it is still important for students to learn that one number is acting on the other.

How to use: We suggest using paper condiment or bathroom cups to represent groups. They hold the small digit sticks well and are easy to come by. When referring to groups at the concrete level, they may be referred to as "cups of" and eventually as "groups of." At the representational and abstract levels, the groups should be referred to as "groups of." For example, $8 \div 2$ should be phrased as "8 objects are split evenly into 2 groups." Since we are dividing or evenly distributing, we are interested in how many per group.

 ## DIVISOR LINE

The divisor line separates the numerator from the denominator. It simply means to divide such that if the numerator were 7 and the denominator were 15, we would say "7 divided by 15." We recommend using a colored paper strip to represent the divisor line.

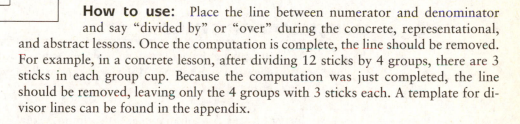

How to use: Place the line between numerator and denominator and say "divided by" or "over" during the concrete, representational, and abstract lessons. Once the computation is complete, the line should be removed. For example, in a concrete lesson, after dividing 12 sticks by 4 groups, there are 3 sticks in each group cup. Because the computation was just completed, the line should be removed, leaving only the 4 groups with 3 sticks each. A template for divisor lines can be found in the appendix.

 ## EQUAL SIGN

Erroneously, young children conclude that "equals" means to solve, when, in fact, it separates two equal parts of a mathematical statement. Using a vertically displayed string is a quick way to separate two or more parts of an equation so that when a computation is added to one side of the equation, it must be computed to the other side.

How to use: Place a string where there would be an equal sign for concrete lessons. For pictorial lessons, draw a curvy line down from the equal sign. A 5-inch cotton string works best, as it lays flat and is easy to manipulate.

 ## POSITIVE, OR PLUS, SYMBOL

For computation, use the plus symbol interchangeably for addition or as a positive symbol. As a positive symbol, it means to the right on a number line. As an addition symbol, it means to combine or group.

How to use: Place the symbol where the addition or positive symbol would be. Use the same language in each of the three stages of learning: concrete, representational, or abstract. A template for the plus symbol can be found in the appendix.

 ## NEGATIVE, OR MINUS, SYMBOL

For computation, use the minus symbol interchangeably for subtraction or as a negative symbol. As a negative symbol, it means to the left on a number line. As a subtraction symbol, it means to remove or reduce.

How to use: Place the symbol where the subtraction or negative symbol would be. Use the same language in each of the three stages of learning: concrete, representational, or abstract. A template for the minus symbol can be found in the appendix.

 ## MULTIPLICATION SYMBOL

To help students recognize when multiplication is occurring, you may wish to use a multiplication symbol. Multiplication can be displayed through parentheses, a dot, or a simple x.

How to use: You may place the symbol where multiplication would be. Use the same language, "groups of," in each of the three stages of learning: concrete, representational, or abstract. A template for the multiplication symbol can be found in the appendix.

 ## VARIABLE OR UNKNOWN

To represent an unknown or a variable while solving equations, we use a letter symbol: X, Y, or N. Obviously, many other options exist and should be explored, but we maintain these three symbols as placeholders for numbers in equations.

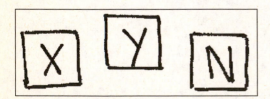

How to use: Use the symbol as it would be used in a numerical sentence (where the unknown is). Use the same language in each of the three stages of learning: concrete, representational, or abstract. A template for each letter can be found in the appendix.

 ## ORGANIZATION OF MATERIALS

Using the materials described above for this intervention requires an organizational system to be in place prior to beginning instruction. When setting up your organization system, try to keep it simple and easy to use for both you and your students.

Each student must have access to a complete set of materials. One cost-effective system we recommend is for each student to have a shoebox or a 1-quart clear re-sealable plastic bag containing all materials. The students can decorate his or her container of materials for easy identification. Although more expensive, you may consider using clear plastic shoebox-size containers because of their durability and ease of storage. We also recommended that you have extra materials available to re-place materials as necessary, due to the wear and tear of day-to-day use.

The materials should be stored in the classroom for easy and quick access when needed; however, materials are not required for the representation and abstract lessons in this intervention. Students will not need to access their containers for every lesson. To reduce possible distractions caused by the materials, we recommend setting up a system to signal students when the lesson requires the materials. For example, the let-ter C can be placed in the corner of the board or beside the day's agenda to signal that the lesson requires the use of their materials. Please keep in mind that there is no one correct way to handle the materials; nonetheless, an organization system is important and can help minimize distractions and maximize instructional time.

WHO CAN USE THIS INTERVENTION?

Solving Equations: An Algebra Intervention is written for both general and special education teachers. The effectiveness of this instructional sequence is supported by research in which certified teachers have provided daily whole-class and/or small group mathematics instruction based on the CRA instructional sequence within and outside of the general education classroom. The CRA instructional sequence can be used to supplement the core mathematics curriculum of at-risk students and as a tar-geted intervention for students with documented math disabilities. The teaching ac-tivities outlined in this manual can complement instructional math programs for students with disabilities and students struggling to learn algebraic or linear equa-tions and functions. It is important to note that *Solving Equations: An Algebra In-tervention* was designed to be fully implemented; results are not likely to be as strong as those obtained in the original research studies if only select parts of the CRA instructional sequence are used. In addition to the information and instruc-tional guidelines provided in this manual, ongoing high-quality professional devel-opment for teachers is important to effectively deliver this program.

HOW TO USE THIS INTERVENTION

This intervention includes 25 carefully sequenced lessons with accompanying scripts and problems. All 25 lessons are teacher-directed lessons and presented in the form of scripts. The lesson scripts were designed as guides to help you implement this inter-vention. In addition to the 25 lessons, there is a transitional lesson (#26) designed to help students learn how to apply solving equations to graphing. Along with the les-sons, this manual contains a pretest assessment, an initial advance organizer lesson, sets of cumulative review problems, a posttest assessment, and a teacher's answer key.

PRETEST ASSESSMENT

The pretest is used for placing students within the intervention sequence. In some cases, students may have some skills and should be placed further within the inter-vention. In other cases, the students may need to start at the first lesson. A maxi-mum score (4 out of 4) on any level subtest places the student at the next lesson. However, in situations in which the student places high in one part and low in an-other, there are some areas of overlap that should be taught. For an example, if a student scores 4 out of 4 in simplifying expressions and 0 out of 4 in one-step equations, the student should start at lessons 6 and continue through the program. Scoring 2 or 3 out of 4 in a section places a student at an abstract lesson in that section. This is because the student already has some understanding of the mathematics and needs additional instruction (abstract level), rather than initial instruction (concrete level).

INSTRUCTIONAL COMPONENTS

INITIAL ADVANCE ORGANIZER LESSON

The advance organizer lesson is intended to introduce the purpose of using this intervention to your students. It also teaches students about the various materials they will be using and what each represents (e.g., a cup represents a group). This initial lesson should be taught prior to lesson 1 and requires the students to have all materials. This lesson could be taught on a different day as lesson 1 or on the same day, depending on the school schedule and learner characteristics.

INSTRUCTIONAL LESSONS

Each of the 25 lessons in this manual follows the same format and present information in a clear, systematic, and explicit approach. We strongly encourage you to become familiar with scripts *prior* to presenting lessons to your students; reading scripts during instructional episodes is discouraged. All 25 lessons contain three main components: (1) model, (2) guided practice, and (3) independent practice.

Model: Each lesson contains a modeling section and includes 2–4 problems. The problems are designed to demonstrate the subskill for the lesson. The scripts were designed keeping in mind that students who struggle with algebra need procedures presented in small, logical steps with multiple demonstrations. The scripts also contain clear and consistent language as well as mathematically correct terminology. Another aspect planned into the scripts is the importance of checking for student understanding through specific and purposeful questioning. If it appears during a lesson that students are confused or not following along, it is recommended to repeat the demonstration problems as necessary.

Guided and Independent Practice: Each lesson contains a section for both guided and independent practice with corresponding problems. This is one of the most important parts of the lesson. Students require well-structured and planned opportunities to practice newly introduced content. Adequate practice is essential and should include both guided and independent practice. Following the scripts in guided practice will allow you to work through several problems together with your students to ensure that they are ready for independent practice.

You may want to spend additional time on the guided practice problems before moving to independent practice. Students who struggle to learn math need more time in guided practice, with a great deal of teacher support. It is beneficial to provide immediate corrections and feedback during the guided practice part of the lesson. It is impossible to develop scripts that can predict all possible scenarios; therefore, you may have to deviate from the scripts. One final note: do not rush or skip guided and independent practice. Students need many opportunities to practice what they are learning. In the long term, students will benefit by spending additional time on this part of the lesson. Rushing students forward will only increase the likelihood of overgeneralization and having misconceptions occur.

POSTTEST ASSESSMENT

Once the intervention is completed, use this assessment to determine the overall success of the student with algebra. A student successfully completed a subskill if he or she receives the maximum score per that section (4 out of 4). However, if the student did not achieve mastery on a subtest, use the chart to guide your reteaching and placement.

If you notice that the student included representational marks on the paper with the abstract notation, do not be alarmed. To determine what level the student is at, interview the student on his or her problem-solving approach. If the student describes the marks in concrete terms, then the student may still be thinking at the concrete level. For example, if he or she describes 5 as the numerator in a fraction as 5 sticks above a divisor line, then the student is thinking concretely. If, however, he or she describes a numerator of 5 by saying "five on the top" or "five in the numerator," then the student may be thinking in abstract terms. A student can still obtain correct answers and be at a level other than abstract. If so, help the student develop fluency through more abstract and verbal think-aloud practice.

 ANSWER KEY

The answer key located at the back of this manual contains answers for all problems used in the pretest and posttest assessments and all 25 instructional lessons. Answers are provided for the examples used in each lesson's model and guided practice as well as answers for the independent practice problems. Since answers during the concrete and representational lessons will be displayed with manipulatives or drawings, a description is provide in terms of cups, sticks, and tally marks.

 LEARNING SHEETS

The learning sheets precede scripts that include all instructional lesson components that follow. For your convenience, learning sheets also appear in the appendix for ease of copying. It is important that all students participating in the instruction have a copy of the learning sheet in front of them so that they can follow along with the lesson and problem solve during the guided practice and independent practice phases of instruction.

Pretest

Subsection	Pretest Score	Where Student Begins
Simplifying Expressions	4 out of 4	Review the next section
	2 out of 4	Lesson #3
	0 out of 4	Lesson #1
One step Inverse Operations	4 out of 4	Review the next section
	2 out of 4	Lesson #8
	0 out of 4	Lesson #6
Two+-step Inverse Operations	4 out of 4	Review the next section
	2 out of 4	Lesson #13
	0 out of 4	Lesson #11
Simplifying and Solving Equations	4 out of 4	Review the next section
	2 out of 4	Lesson #18
	0 out of 4	Lesson #16
Transformational Equations	4 out of 4	Review the next section
	2 out of 4	Lesson #23
	0 out of 4	Lesson #21

Pretest

Name: _____

Section A: Simplifying expressions

a) $4U(5) - W + 2W$ b) $-3P + 7 + P - 12$

c) $8 - 2(X + 4) + 2X$ d) $8A + 4B - 4(2A) - 12$

Section B: One-step inverse operations

a) $16 = \dfrac{4F}{6}$ b) $11 = -3C$

c) $3X = 28$ d) $\dfrac{K}{7} = 6$

Section C: Two+-step inverse operations

a) $\dfrac{44}{K} = 11$ b) $2 + \dfrac{1P}{2} = 22$

c) $2 = \dfrac{2M}{5}$ d) $19 = -10 - D$

Section D: Simplifying and solving equations

a) $9 = -Y - 8Y$ b) $12N - 5N - 5 = 13 + 10$

c) $\dfrac{10}{K} = \dfrac{35}{7}$ d) $10F - F + 1F - 4 = 36$

Section E: Transformational equations

a) $8F - 16 = 2F + 26$ b) $11 - 5C = -22 + 6C$

c) $2N - 8 = \dfrac{1N}{2} - 2$ d) $\dfrac{P}{2} + 2 = 2P - 8$

Posttest

Subsection	Posttest Score	Reteach From This Lesson
Simplifying Expressions	4 out of 4	Subskill mastered
	2 out of 4	Lesson #4
	0 out of 4	Lesson #1
One-step Inverse Operations	4 out of 4	Subskill mastered
	2 out of 4	Lesson #8
	0 out of 4	Lesson #6
Two+-step Inverse Operations	4 out of 4	Subskill mastered
	2 out of 4	Lesson #13
	0 out of 4	Lesson #11
Simplifying and Solving Equations	4 out of 4	Subskill mastered
	2 out of 4	Lesson #18
	0 out of 4	Lesson #16
Transformational Equations	4 out of 4	Subskill mastered
	2 out of 4	Lesson #23
	0 out of 4	Lesson #21

Posttest

Name: _____

Section A: Simplifying expressions

a) $3U(8) - G + 2G$ b) $-3N + 7 + N - 12$

c) $7 - 3(Y + 4) + 2Y$ d) $8C + 4H - 4(2C) - 12$

Section B: One-step inverse operations

a) $10 = \dfrac{3V}{6}$ b) $11 = -2X$

c) $3W = 28$ d) $\dfrac{B}{7} = 6$

Section C: Two+-step inverse operations

a) $\dfrac{44}{R} = 11$ b) $2 + \dfrac{1A}{2} = 22$

c) $2 = \dfrac{2T}{5}$ d) $-9 = -10 + W$

Section D: Simplifying and solving equations

a) $9 = -G - 8G$ b) $12Y - 5Y - 5 = 13 + 10$

c) $\dfrac{10}{P} = \dfrac{35}{7}$ d) $10X - X + 1X - 4 = 36$

Section E: Transformational equations

a) $8A - 16 = 2A + 26$ b) $11 - 5N = -22 + 6N$

c) $2X - 8 = \dfrac{1X}{2} - 2$ d) $\dfrac{1K}{2} + 2 = 2K - 8$

Student **LESSON # 1**

Concrete/Hands-on: Simplifying by Combining Like Terms

Describe and Model

    a) $1N + 7 + 2N - 5$ b) $X + 3 - 6$

Guided Practice

    c) $3Y + Y + 2$ d) $-N + N + 5$

    e) $\dfrac{1N}{2} - 4 + 5$ f) $10 - 2X - 3X$

Independent Practice

    g) $N + N + 6$ h) $5 + 2N + 2$

    i) $3Y + 4 + 2Y$ j) $-X - 2X + 3$

Problem Solving

    k) While cleaning up your room, you find 3 books (3) and (+) two bags of books (2Y) under your bed. Then on the floor you see 6 more books (+6). Set up the simplest expression and show how many books you found.

    l) In PE, the teacher throws out 5 balls (5), 2 sacks of balls (2N), and then 3 more balls (+3). Set up the simplest equation and show how many balls there were in PE.

Teaching LESSON # 1

Concrete/Hands-on: Simplifying by Combining Like Terms

Welcome: Today we will learn a new approach to solving equations. We are going to start with simplifying expressions.

Social Relevance: The reason it is important to learn to simplify expressions is because this skill will help you make seemingly complicated things easier to see and work with. For example, if I have 3 cups and 2 hot dogs and my friend has 4 hot dogs and 2 cups, I know that when we are talking about what *we* have, it makes more sense to say, "Together, we have 6 hot dogs and 5 cups" rather than listing individually what we each have.

Academic Relevance: In math, this same concept of simplifying matters works well when equations get really long. Discovering what is essential in equations and expressions helps make doing math more efficient.

Let's get started: Today we will work with hands-on materials. This step helps us understand the steps that we need to solve the problems.

Model

In problem 1a), $1N + 7 + 2N - 5$, I am going to set up the expression just as we see it.

Now I am going to separate out the expression per addend, such that the unknown signs are on their own line and the integers are on another. I place a positive sign in front of the 1N. I know that it is positive, but this is a good habit when problems become more complex.

Next, I calculate the number of coefficients per unknown. I have 1 cup of N and 2 cups of N, both positive. The gives me +3 cups of N. Then I calculate integers. I have +7 − 5. That equals +2. The answer is +3N + 2.

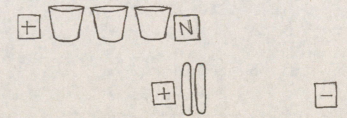

In problem 1b), X + 3 − 6, I am going to set up the expression just as we see it.

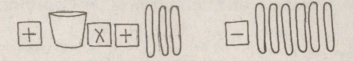

Now I am going to separate out the expression per addend, such that the unknown signs are on their own line and the integers are on another. For X, there is an implied 1 for the coefficient in front of the X. So I will place a + and 1 cup there.

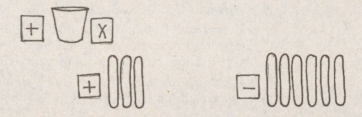

Next I calculate the number of coefficients per unknown. There is only 1 cup of X, so I leave it alone. Then I calculate integers. I have +3 sticks and −6 sticks. These numbers go in opposite directions on a number line, so I pull out an equal number of sticks each (3). That leaves −3. I am left with +1X + −3.

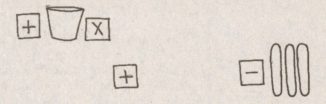

Guided Practice

For this section, I will start working one step at a time with you. By the end, you will be leading me one step at a time.

For problems 1c) and 1d):

- How do we start?—solicit answer
- What do we do next?—solicit answer
- What should we group first?—solicit answer
- What should we group next?—solicit answer
- What is the answer?—solicit answer

For problems 1e) and 1f):

- Show me what to do first.
- Now show me what happens next.
- What do you do now?
- What is your answer?

Independent Practice

Try the next four on your own. When you are done with all four, we will check them as a group.

Word Problems

Let's try to complete these two word problems together.

1k) Read the problem. What is the problem asking for? Yes, the number of books. So each variable must lead to the number of books. What do we know from the problem? We are given the symbols in this problem. Let's make sense of them. *Go through each of the symbol sets and describe the relationship of each:*

3 books means 3 because the answer is in number of books.

And means + because we are putting things together.

2 bags of books means 2Y, which means Y represent a bag of books. We do not know how many are in each bag, so we call them Y.

6 more books means to add 6 because "more" means we are putting more books into the total.

Which parts do we combine? Yes, combine the parts that have like terms.

What do we end up with? *Have students concretely answer the problem.*

Yes, 2 bags of books (2Y) and 9 more books.

1l) Read the problem. What is the problem asking for? Yes, the number of balls in PE. So each variable must lead to the number of balls. What do we know from the problem? We are given the symbols in this problem. Let's make sense of them. *Go through each of the symbol sets and describe the relationship of each:*

Why 5? Yes, because there are 5 balls.

What does 2N stand for? Yes, 2 sacks of balls. N stands for each sack of balls.

Why is there a +3? Yes, 3 more balls.

Which ones do we combine? Yes, the ones that have like terms.

What do we end up with? *Have students concretely answer the problem.*

Yes, 2 sacks of balls (2N) and 8 more books.

Student **LESSON # 2**

Representations/Pictures

Describe/Model

a) $2N - 2X + 12 + X$ b) $3H - 5N - 2$

Guided Practice

c) $4N - \dfrac{2X}{3} + N - 7$ d) $T - 3T + 2T + 2$

e) $4 - 3X + 3 + Y$ f) $-6 + T + 4T + 2$

Independent Practice

g) $4U + 5U - W + 2W$ h) $6P + 4 - 3P + 7$

i) $3X + 4Y + 14 - 4X$ j) $2L + 6W - 2L + 13$

Problem Solving

k) You can carry only so many books. One teacher gives you 2 big books (2B) and 4 small books (4L) along with 4 pieces of paper (4) to carry. Your next teacher gives you 2 more big books (2B) to carry home. Set up the simplest expression to show how many books and pieces of paper you have to carry.

l) You are helping make a cake and icing. The cake takes 2 cups of flour (2F) and 1 cup of sugar (1X). The icing takes 2 cups of sugar (2X) and 1 cup of water (1W). What are the total ingredients? Set up the simplest expression to solve the problem.

Teaching LESSON # 2

Representations/Pictures

Let's get started. Today we will draw pictures of expressions similarly to how we simplified them yesterday. By learning to draw pictures, you will be able to rationalize some of the more difficult problems to come.

Model

In problem 2a), 2N − 2X + 12 + X, I am going to set up the expression just as we see it. I draw 1 cup in front of the last X because there is an implied coefficient of 1.

Now I am going to separate out the expression per addend, such that the unknown signs are on their own line and the integers are on another.

Next, I calculate the number of coefficients per unknown. There is only one set of N, so the 2N remains. For X, I have −2 and +1. I can cross out an equal number from each to reveal that −1 remains. So, I have −1X. Then I calculate integers. The 12 is alone, so I leave it alone. I am left with 2N, −1X, and 12. The answer is 2N − 1X + 12.

In problem 2b), 3H − 5N − 2, I am going to set up the expression just as we see it.

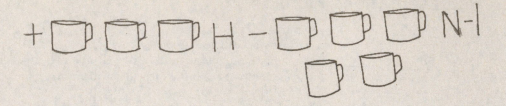

Now I am going to separate out the expression per addend, such that the unknown signs are on their own line and the integers are on another.

Next I calculate the number of coefficients per unknown. However, each unknown has only one coefficient. Then I am to calculate the integers. However, it is alone as well. I am left with 3H − 5N − 2.

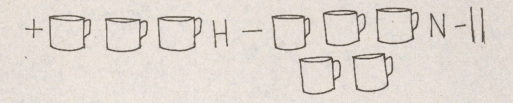

Guided Practice

For this section, I will start working one step at a time with you. By the end, you will be leading me one step at a time.

For problems 2c) and 2d):

- How do we start?—solicit answer
- What do we do next?—solicit answer
- What should we group first?—solicit answer
- What should we group next?—solicit answer
- What is the answer?—solicit answer

For problems 2e) and 2f):

- Show me what to do first.
- Now show me what happens next.
- What do you do now?
- What is your answer?

Independent Practice

Try the next four on your own. When you are done with all four, we will check them as a group.

Word Problems

Let's try to complete these two word problems together.

1k) Read the problem. What is the problem asking for? Yes, the number of books you have to carry home. So each variable must lead to the number of books. What do we know from the problem? We are given some of the symbols here. Let's make sense of them and see what is missing. *Go through each of the symbol sets and describe the relationship of each:*

Why 2B? Yes, because there are 2 big books.

Is there an operational term here? Yes, *and* means to add.

What does 2L stand for? Yes, two little books.

Is there another word that shows an operation? Yes, *along with* means to add again.

The 4 stands for what? Yes, 4 pieces of paper.

Is there another operational term? Yes. The term *more* both imply addition..

Finally, why 2B at the end? Yes, 2 big books.

What do we end up with? *Have students pictorially answer the problem.*

Yes, 4 big books, 2 little books, and 4 pieces of paper.

1l) Read the problem. What is the problem asking for? Yes, some ingredients to make a cake and icing. Each variable must lead to the ingredients. What do we know from the problem? We are given some of the symbols here. Let's make sense of them and see what is missing. *Go through each of the symbol sets and describe the relationship of each:*

Why 2F? Yes, because there are 2 cups of flour.

Is there an operational term here? Yes, *and* means to add.

What does 1X stand for? Yes, 1 cup of sugar.

Is there another term that shows an operation? Yes, *takes with* means to add again.

What does the 2X stand for? Yes, 2 cups of sugar.

Is there another operational term? Yes, *and* means to add.

Finally, what does the 1W mean? Yes, 1 cup of water.

What do we end up with? *Have students pictorially answer the problem.*

Yes, we have 2 cups of flour, 3 cups of sugar, and 1 cup of water.

Student **LESSON # 3**

Abstract

Describe/Model

a) $8 - 3F + 2(3X)$

b) $3(X + 2) + X + 1$

Guided Practice

c) $-N + 4K + 2W + 2N$

d) $\dfrac{24Z}{6} + 6 + Z$

e) $\dfrac{7}{H} + 3P - \dfrac{1}{2} - K$

f) $-5N + 5 - 5N + 10 + C$

Independent Practice

g) $4U(5) - W + 2W$

h) $-3P + 7 + P - 12$

i) $\dfrac{12W}{3} + 4 - 12$

j) $2W + 6 - 2K + 2K$

k) $6X(4) + 14 - 4X$

l) $2B - 2W - 12 + 10$

Problem Solving

m) Your uncle brought 4 red presents and 2 blue presents to the party. Your little brother then took 2 blue presents. Aunt Patty brought 2 more red presents. Set up the expression to figure out how many presents were left.

n) The football team passed the ball for 5 yards and then ran for 4 yards. They passed for 10 yards more and then ran for a loss of 2 yards. Set up the expression to show how many yards were gained by the team through running and passing.

Teaching **LESSON # 3**

Abstract: Simplifying by Combining Like Terms

Welcome: Today we will use what we did with hands-on and picture lessons, but we will do it using numbers today.

Relevance: We learned how to combine like terms and how to recognize like terms from unlike terms. We will take those lessons and now go a bit faster by using similar procedures to those used previously.

Let's get started:

Model

a) 1. Separate the addends of this expression by their variable per row.
 2. Do we have any calculations to do? Let's start by multiplying 2 by 3X. We now have 6X. Any more calculations? Addition and subtraction? Good.
 3. Simplify the expression.
 4. What are we left with?

b) 1. Separate the addends of this expression by their variable per row.
 2. Do we have any calculations to do? Yes, let's multiply 3 by X + 2. We now have 3X + 6. Any more calculations? Addition and subtraction? Good.

 Note: If students do not know the distributive property, please show how this calculation is accurate.

 3. Simplify the expression.
 4. What are we left with?

Guided Practice

For this section, I will start working one step at a time with you. By the end, you will be leading me one step at a time.
 For problems 3c) and 3d):

Separate addends by their variable per row.

Complete calculations.

Simplify the expression.

Provide answer.

 For problems 3e) and 3f):

Follow the same procedures but have the student tell you the steps ahead of time. Assess student knowledge of the procedures.

Independent Practice

Try the next six on your own. When you are done with all six, we will check them as a group.

Word Problems

Let's try to complete these two word problems together.

1k) Read the problem.

 What is the problem asking for?

 What do we know from the problem? *Go through each of the symbol sets and operations in the expression.*

Write out what we have in the problem.

Which parts do we combine?

What do we end up with? *Have students answer the problem.*

1l) Read the problem.

What is the problem asking for?

What do we know from the problem? *Go through each of the symbol sets and operations in the expression.*

Write out what we have in the problem.

Which parts do we combine?

What do we end up with? *Have students answer the problem.*

Student   LESSON # 4

Abstract

Describe/Model

    a) $5X + 12K - 7X + 5$ b) $3W + 6(3 - G)$

Guided Practice

    c) $Y + 4Z + 5 - 3Y + 8$ d) $\frac{1}{2}(8A - 4A) + 5A$

Independent Mixed Practice

    e) $3Y + 4 + 2Y$ f) $3V - 5T + 5V - 3$

    g) $8 - 2(X + 4) + 2X$ h) $8A + 4B - 4(2A) - 12$

    i) $9M - 6R + 7(R - 2M)$ j) $X + 18 + 20X - 4$

4k) To build a house you need supplies. You bring 3 bundles of wood and 5 pallets of bricks. The foreman brings an additional 10 pallets of bricks and 5 bundles of wood. Set up a simple expression to show what was brought.

4l) A parking company wants to estimate its income for the day. The company owns 2 parking garages and 1 parking lot. Each parking garage has 4 floors where there are 30 cars per floor. The parking lot has 20 cars. Set up a simple expression to help the company calculate the total income. Explain your rationale.

Teaching **LESSON # 4**

Abstract: Simplifying by Combining Like Terms

Welcome: Today we will continue simplifying expressions like we did previously. Only now, the problems are more difficult.

Relevance: We learned how to combine like terms and how to recognize like terms from unlike terms. We will take those lessons and now go a bit faster by using procedures we have used previously.

Let's get started:

Model

a) 1. Separate the addends of this expression by their variable per row.
2. Do we have any calculations to do? Just addition and subtraction.
3. Simplify the expression. We have two addends with X. What is $5X - 7X$? Yes, $-2X$.
4. What is the answer? $-2X + 12K + 5$

b) 1. Separate the addends of this expression by their variable per row.
2. Do we have any calculations to do? We must multiply 6 by $(3 - G)$. What do find? Yes, $18 - 6G$. Any more calculations? Just addition and subtraction.
3. Simplify the expression. No like terms, so what are we left with?
4. What is the answer? $3W + 18 - 6G$.

Guided Practice

For this section, I will start working one step at a time with you. By the end, you will be leading me one step at a time.

For problem 4c):

Separate addends by their variable per row.

Complete calculations.

Simplify the expression.

Provide answer.

For problem 4d):

Follow the same procedures but have the student tell you the steps ahead of time. Assess student knowledge of the procedures.

Independent Practice

Try the next six on your own. When you are done with all six, we will check them as a group.

Word Problems

Try to complete these two word problems independently.

Remember the steps:

What is the problem asking for?

What do we know from the problem? *Go through each of the symbol sets and operations in the expression.*

Write out what we have in the problem.

Which parts do we combine?

What do we end up with? *Have students answer the problem.*

Student   **LESSON # 5**

Fluency/Work Fast

Simplify the following

a) $6Y + 14 - 8Y + 1$ b) $3CM - 7IN + 9CM - 3IN$

c) $-2(X + 1) + 20$ d) $3A + 3A - 3A(2) - B$

e) $9M - 6R + 7(R - 2M)$ f) $4N + 18 + 20X - 4X$

g) $4R + 12R + 5 - R$ h) $3Y - 5X + 5Z - 3$

i) $2H + 2(H + H) + 3$ j) $8F + 4G - 2G - 12F$

k) $5 + 13(X + 1)$ l) $N + 3 + 20N - 4R$

m) $19 - 9K + 12 - W$ n) $1/3(6X + 15) + X$

o) $3Y + 4 + 2Y$ p) $2DM + 5KM + 8 - 2KM$

Teaching **LESSON # 5**

Fluency/Work Fast

Now that you have shown that you know how to simplify expressions, let's see how many accurate answers you can give in a 2-minute timed quiz. The problems in this quiz are mixed up, so read each problem carefully. We will start with this one. *(Point to any problem on the sheet.)* Once you give an answer, do not stop; go to the next question on the sheet to the right, or return to the next line below. Answer every question. If you skip a question, that counts as incorrect. If you happen to come to the last problem on the sheet, go to the problem at the top of the paper and do not stop. *(Run finger across and down the lines of problems to read like a paragraph.)* I will stop you 2 minutes after I say go.

Ready? Go.

(Total student correct and incorrect addends during the 2 minutes on a separate sheet of paper. Upon completion, tell the students what you tallied and have each student graph his or her performance. You may want to talk about the growth of the students' performance between lessons.)

Post these steps and teach them. These will provide the basis for solving simple equations for the rest of the lessons.

ISOLATE is a stepwise approach to solving equations spelling out each step the students must complete, thereby helping the student work through problems in a logical sequence (Witzel et al., 2003). The goal is to locate the variable and determine what is happening on each side of the equal sign. Then, decide calculations to isolate the variable on one side of the equal sign and conclude with what is on the other. For equation solving in the next sections, you will use ISOLATE.

I—Identify the variable to be solved; point to the variable.

S—Set up calculations to isolate the variable (make the coefficient one with no addends).

O—Organize the calculations to balance across the equal sign.

L—List the calculations to happen in the same order on both sides.

A—Answer the calculations on the variable's side first.

T—Total the calculations on the other side of the equation.

E—Evaluate that the answer is accurate.

Note: Only cover them up after the students have learned them.

Student **LESSON # 6**

Concrete/Hands-on: Solving Inverse Operations (One-Step Equations)

Describe/Model

a) $1X = 3$

b) $-8 = 4X$

c) $\dfrac{N}{2} = 2$

d) $\dfrac{1Y}{3} = 4$

Guided Practice

e) $6 = -3Y$

f) $\dfrac{N}{4} = 2$

g) $3 = \dfrac{1X}{3}$

h) $2N = 12$

Independent Practice

i) $10 = 2Y$

j) $7 = \dfrac{X}{2}$

k) $3N = 9$

l) $\dfrac{Y}{3} = -1$

Problem Solving

m) In a basketball game, three players (3X) scored (=) 15 points together. What is the average amount of points that each scored?

    1. Set up the equation.
    2. Answer the equation.

n) Frank sold cell phones. If he sold 4 cell phones (4N) he made (=) $12. How much did he make per cell phone? Let N = cost per phone.

    1. Set up the equation.
    2. Answer the equation.

Teaching **LESSON # 6**

Concrete/Hands-on: Solving Inverse Operations (One-Step Equations)

Purpose: When we simplified expressions, we tried to find out what was essential about each expression. Solving for unknowns is similar. We want to find out what the variable stands for. In these lessons, it will always be a number. However, as you advance in math, you will use the same steps to solve for an unknown, and you will have unknowns in the answer.

Relevance: When you are given a problem to solve, you will work to find the answer. In these problems, a problem is given such that a number is unknown. We will work together to find the answers.

Note: Fractions will be calculated here. Show why and how this works. To make this more systematic, calculate the denominator first and then calculate the numerator.

Let's get started:

Describe/Model

6a) Let's set up the problem as it is written: $1X = 3$.

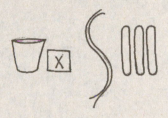

I—I want to solve for X, so I need to find out what is in 1 cup, the coefficient, of X.

S—There are no other calculations on the same side as X, so I will divide each side of the equation by 1 cup.

O—I place a divisor line and 1 cup on both sides

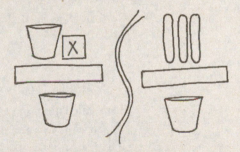

L—Let's calculate.

A—Answer the unknown side: 1 divided by 1 is 1.

T—Total the other side: 3 sticks in 1 cup is 1 cup of 3 sticks, or 3 sticks per cup.

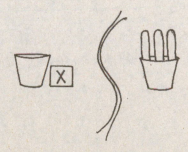

E—The answer is 1X = 3.

6b) Let's set up the problem as it is written: −8 = 4X.

I—I want to solve for X, so I need to find out what is in 1 cup, the coefficient, of X.

S—There is no other number aside from the coefficient on the same side as X, so I will divide each side of the equation by 4 cups.

O—I place a divisor line and 4 cups on both sides.

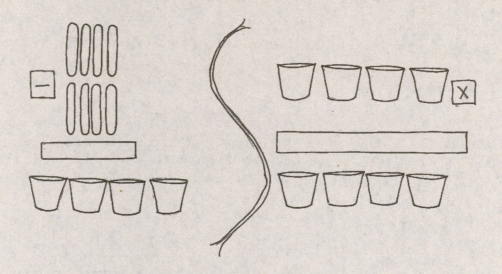

L—Let's calculate.

A—Answer the unknown side: 4 divided by 4 is 1.

T—Total the other side: 8 sticks equally divided into 4 cups is 2 sticks per cup. Also, a negative sign remains.

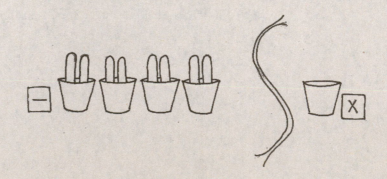

E—The answer is −2 = 1X, or 1X = −2.

6c) Let's set up the problem as it is written: N/2 = 2.

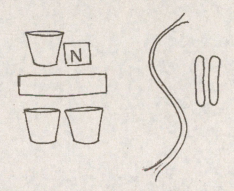

I—I want to solve for N, so I need to find out what is in 1 cup of N.

S—There is no other number aside from the coefficient on the same side as N, so I will work with the coefficient, 1/2. Even though the 1 does not show, just like in the previous lessons, there is an implied 1 next to each unknown. Since N is divided by 2, I multiply each side of the equation by 2 cups. Then, I divide each side by 1.

O—I place 2 cups divided by 1 cup on both sides.

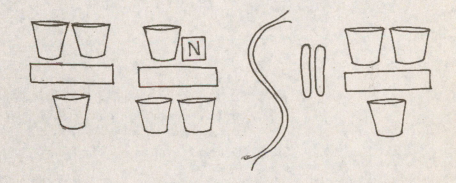

L—Let's calculate.

A—Answer the unknown side: 2 divided by 2 is 1, and 1 divided by 1 is 1. I have 1N.

T—Total the other side: 2 cups of 2 sticks each is 4 sticks total. I lay down the 4 sticks. Now, let's divide the 4 sticks by 1 cup.

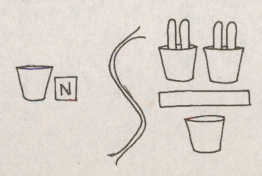

E—The answer is 4 sticks per cup, or 1N = 4.

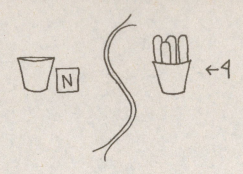

6d) Let's set up the problem as it is written: 1Y/3 = 4.

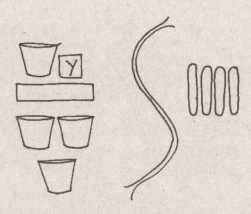

I—I want to solve for Y, so I need to find out what is in 1 cup of Y.

S—There is no other number aside from the coefficient on the same side as Y, so I will work with the coefficient, 1/3. First, I will multiply each side by 3 cups. Then, I will divide each side by 1 cup.

O—I place 3 cups divided by 1 cup on both sides.

L—Let's calculate.

A—Answer the unknown side: 3 divided by 3 is 1, and 1 divided by 1 is 1. Thus, I have 1Y.

T—Total the other side: 3 cups of 4 sticks each is 12 sticks total. I lay down the 12 sticks. Now, I divide the 12 sticks into 1 cup. It is very tight fit, but I have 12 sticks in the 1 cup.

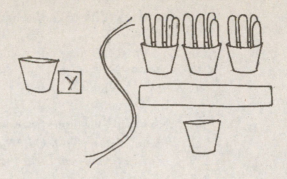

E—The answer is 12 sticks per cup, or 1Y = 12.

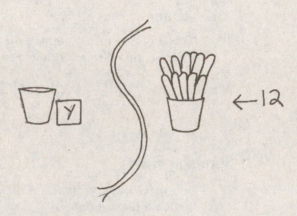

Guided Practice

In this section, I will go through the steps for the first two and you will complete them with me step-by-step. By the last two, you will work at least one step ahead of me.

Go through each step by asking what to do and doing it as close to simultaneously with the students as possible.

6e) 6 = −3Y

I—I want to solve for what variable?

S—There is no other number aside from the coefficient on the same side as Y, so I will work with the coefficient, −3. I will divide each side by 3 cups and a negative sign.

O—What do I place on both sides?

L—Let's calculate.

A—Answer the unknown side: −3 divided by −3 is 1. Thus, I have 1Y.

T—Total the other side: 6 sticks into 3 cups is what? Yes, 2 sticks per cup. What sign is left over? Yes, the negative.

E—The answer is what? Yes, 1Y = −2 sticks per cup, or −2.

6f) $\frac{N}{4} = 2$

I—I want to solve for N, so I need to find out what is in 1 cup of N.

S—There is no other number aside from the coefficient on the same side as Y, so I will work with the coefficient, 1/4. First, I will multiply each side by 4 cups. Then, I will divide each side by 1 cup.

O—I place 4 cups divided by 1 cup on both sides.

L—Let's calculate.

A—Answer the unknown side: 4 divided by 4 is 1, and 1 divided by 1 is 1. Thus, I have 1N.

T—Total the other side: 4 cups of 2 sticks each is 8 sticks total. I lay down the 8 sticks. Now, I divide the 8 sticks into 1 cup. It is very tight fit, but I have 8 sticks in the 1 cup.

E—The answer is what? 12 sticks per cup, or 1Y = 12.

Now it is your turn to work one step ahead of me.

For g) and h), go through ISOLATE one step at a time, having students perform the step first. Then, check their work and go accordingly.

g) $3 = \dfrac{1X}{3}$

h) N2 = 12

Independent Practice

Now it is your turn. Complete these four problems on your own concretely. I will be walking around to assess how you are doing but not necessarily to help.

i) 10 = 2Y

j) $7 = \dfrac{X}{2}$

k) 3N = 9

l) $\dfrac{Y}{3} = -1$

Problem Solving

Let's try a couple of these together.
Read the problem.

m) In a basketball game, three players (3X) scored (=) 15 points together. What is the average amount of points that each scored?
1. Set up the equation. Explain your reasoning.
2. Answer the equation. What is the answer? Does it make sense, and why?

Read the problem.

n) Frank sold cell phones. If he sold 4 cell phones (4N) he made (=) $12. How much did he make per cell phone? Let N = cost per phone.
1. Set up the equation. Explain your reasoning.
2. Answer the equation. What is your answer? Does it make sense, and why?

Student **LESSON # 7**

Representational/Pictures (One-Step Equations)

Describe/Model

    a) $7 = -T$ b) $12 = 4Y$

    c) $3 = \dfrac{X}{6}$ d) $\dfrac{2C}{3} = 2$

Guided Practice

    e) $2 = H$ f) $\dfrac{W}{4} = 3$

    g) $-3F = 6$ h) $5 = \dfrac{1X}{3}$

Independent Practice

    i) $4P = 16$ j) $14 = -2T$

    k) $25 = 5Y$ l) $10 = -2X$

    m) $-3 = \dfrac{N}{5}$ n) $\dfrac{1P}{2} = 4$

Problem Solving

    o) Carl (C) had a large number of chocolates. He split ($\div$) them among 5 friends. After he split them ($=$), each friend had 2 chocolates. How many did he have total? Set up the equation and solve.

Teaching LESSON # 7

Representational/Pictures (One-Step Equations)

Describe/Model

Purpose: When we simplified expressions, we tried to find out what was essential about each expression. Solving for unknowns is similar. We want to find out what the variable stands for. In these lessons, it will always be a number. However, as you advance in math, you will use the same steps to solve for an unknown, and you will have unknowns in the answer.

Relevance: When you are given a problem to solve, you will work to find the answer. In these problems, a problem is given such that a number is unknown. We will work together to find the answers.

Let's get started:

Describe/Model

7a) Let's set up the problem as it is written: $7 = -T$.

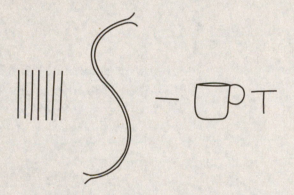

I—I want to solve for T, so I need to find out what is in 1, the coefficient, of T. So, I draw a − and one group of T.

S—There is no other calculations on the same side as T, so I will divide each side of the equation by −1 group.

O—I draw a divisor line and a negative sign and 1 group on both sides.

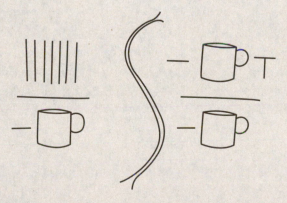

L—Let's calculate.

A—Answer the unknown side: 1 divided by 1 is 1. Negative divided by negative is positive. So I draw that in.

T—Total the other side: 7 goes in 1 group. Also, the negative sign remains.

E—The answer is 1T = −7.

7b) Let's set up the problem as it is written: 12 = 4Y.

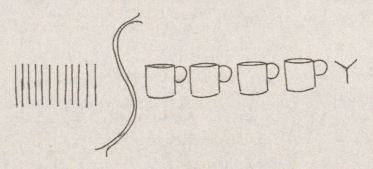

I—I want to solve for Y, so I need to find out what is in 1 group of Y.

S—There is no other number aside from the coefficient on the same side as Y, so I will divide each side of the equation by 4 groups.

O—I draw a divisor line and 4 groups on both sides.

L—Let's calculate.

A—Answer the unknown side: 4 divided by 4 is 1. I cross them.

T—Total the other side: 12 equally divided into 4 groups is 3 per group. I draw it as such.

E—The answer is 3 = 1Y, or 1Y = 3.

7c) Let's set up the problem as it is written: 3 = 1X/6.

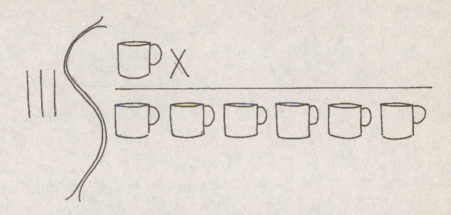

I—I want to solve for X, so I need to find out what is in 1 group of X.

S—There is no other number aside from the coefficient on the same side as X, so I will work with the coefficient, 1/6. Since X is divided by 6, I multiply each side of the equation by 6 groups. Then, I divide each side by 1.

O—I draw 6 groups divided by 1 group on both sides.

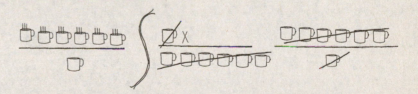

L—Let's calculate.

A—Answer the unknown side: 6 divided by 6 is 1, and 1 divided by 1 is 1. I have 1X.

T—Total the other side: 6 groups of 3 is 18 total. I draw a circle around all 18. Now, let's divide the 18 by 1 group. 18 divided by 1 is 18.

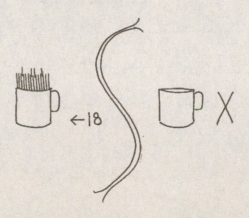

E—The answer is 18, or 1X = 18.

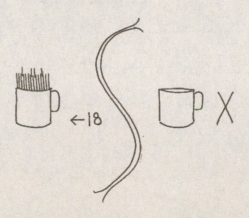

7d) Let's set up the problem as it is written: 2Y/3 = 2.

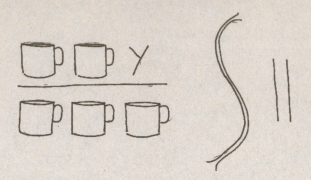

I—I want to solve for Y, so I need to find out what is in 1 cup of Y.

S—There is no other number aside from the coefficient on the same side as Y, so I will work with the coefficient, 2/3. First, I will multiply each side by 3 groups. Then, I will divide each side by 2 groups.

O—I draw 3 groups divided by 2 groups on both sides.

L—Let's calculate.

A—Answer the unknown side: 3 divided by 3 is 1, and 2 divided by 2 is 1. Thus, I have 1Y. I cross them.

T—Total the other side: 3 groups of 2 sticks each is 6 total. I draw the tallies per group and circle the total number, since it is multiplication. Now, I divide the 6 tallies into 2 groups. 6 tallies divided into 2 groups is 3 tallies per group. I draw them into the groups.

E—The answer is 3 per group, or 1Y = 2.

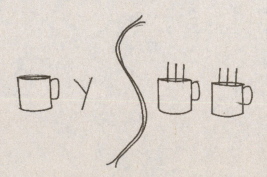

Guided Practice

In this section, I will go through the steps for the first two and you will complete them with me step-by-step. By the last two, you will work at least one step ahead of me.

Go through each step by asking what to do and doing it as close to simultaneously with the students as possible.

7e) $2 = H$

> I—I want to solve for what variable?
>
> S—There is no other number aside from the coefficient on the same side as H, so I will work with the coefficient, 1. I will divide each side by 1 group.
>
> O—What do I place on both sides?
>
> L—Let's calculate.
>
> A—Answer the unknown side: 1 divided by 1 is 1. Thus, I have 1H.
>
> T—Total the other side: 2 tallies into 1 group is what? Yes, 2 tallies per group.
>
> E—The answer is what? Yes, 1H = 2 tallies per group, or 2.

7f) $\dfrac{W}{4} = 3$

> I—I want to solve for W, so I need to find out what is in 1 cup of W.
>
> S—There is no other number aside from the coefficient on the same side as Y, so I will work with the coefficient, 1/4. First, I will multiply each side by 4 groups. Then, I will divide each side by 1 group.
>
> O—I place 4 groups divided by 1 group on both sides.
>
> L—Let's calculate.
>
> A—Answer the unknown side: 4 divided by 4 is 1, and 1 divided by 1 is 1. Thus, I have 1W.
>
> T—Total the other side: 4 groups of 3 tallies each is 12 tallies total. I write 12 tallies. Now, I divide the 12 tallies into 1 group.
>
> E—The answer is what? 12 tallies per group, or 1W = 12.
>
> Now it is your turn to work one step ahead of me.

For g) and h), go through ISOLATE one step at a time, having students perform the step first. Then, check their work and go accordingly.

g) $-3F = 6$

h) $5 = \dfrac{1X}{3}$

Independent Practice

Now it is your turn. Complete these six problems on your own pictorially without help. I will be walking around to assess how you are doing but not necessarily to help.

i) $4P = 16$ j) $14 = -2T$

k) $25 = 5Y$ l) $10 = -2X$

m) $-3 = \dfrac{N}{5}$ n) $\dfrac{1P}{2} = 7$

Problem Solving

Try this word problem.
    Read the problem.

o) Carl (C) had a large number of chocolates. He split (÷) them among 5 friends. After he split them (=), each friend had 2 chocolates. How many did he have total?

1. Set up the equation. Explain your reasoning.
2. Answer the equation using ISOLATE. Show all of your work. What is the answer? Does it make sense, and why?

Student   **LESSON # 8**

Abstract

Describe/Model

a) $8 = -2Y$

b) $\dfrac{2W}{4} = 11$

Guided Practice

c) $-27 = 9P$

d) $6 = \dfrac{3X}{5}$

Independent Practice

e) $P = -8$

f) $-14 = 14M$

g) $16 = \dfrac{4F}{6}$

h) $11 = -C$

i) $81 = \dfrac{9D}{9}$

j) $8 = \dfrac{U}{5}$

k) $63 = 9Y$

l) $8 = -4W$

Problem Solving

m) Al's backpack could carry 5 books. How many backpacks would Al need to carry 25 books? Set up the equation and solve.

Teaching LESSON # 8
Abstract

Describe/Model

Purpose: Solving equations using hands-on and pictorial methods taught the procedures for solving equations. Now we are going to go a little faster. Instead of using concrete and pictorial ways to solve for the variable, we are going to write out the numbers and solve the equations abstractly.

Let's get started.

Describe/Model

8a) Let's set up the problem as it is written: $8 = -2Y$.

I—I want to solve for Y, so I need to find out what is in 1 Y.

S—There are no other calculations on the same side as Y, so I will divide each side of the equation by -2.

O—I draw a divisor line and -2 on both sides.

L—Let's calculate.

A—Answer the unknown side: -2 divided by -2 is 1. So I have 1Y.

T—Total the other side: 8 divided by -2 is -4.

E—The answer is $1Y = -4$.

8b) Let's set up the problem as it is written: $2W/4 = 11$.

I—I want to solve for W, so I need to find out what is in 1 W.

S—There is no other number aside from the coefficient on the same side as W, so I will divide each side of the equation by 2 and multiply both sides by 4.

O—I draw a divisor line with 4 in the numerator and 2 in the denominator on both sides.

L—Let's calculate.

A—Answer the unknown side: 2 divided by 2 is 1, and 4 divided by 4 is 1. I am left with 1W.

T—Total the other side: 11 times 4 is 44. Next, 44 divided by 2 is 22.

E—The answer is $1W = 22$.

Guided Practice

In this section, I will go through the steps for the first one and you will complete it with me step-by-step. For the last one, you will work at least one step ahead of me.

Go through each step by asking what to do and doing it as close to simultaneously with the students as possible.

8c) $-27 = 9P$

I—I want to solve for what variable?

S—What is the coefficient, and what should I do next?

O—What do I place on both sides?

L—Let's calculate.

A—Answer the unknown side.

T—Total the other side.

E—The answer is what? Yes, $1P = -3$.

Now it is your turn to work one step ahead of me.

For d), go through ISOLATE one step at a time, having students perform the step first. Then, check their work and go accordingly.

8d) $6 = 3X/5$

Independent Practice

Now it is your turn. Complete these eight problems on your own pictorially without help. I will be walking around to assess how you are doing but not necessarily to help.

e) $P = -8$

f) $-14 = 14M$

g) $16 = \dfrac{4F}{6}$

h) $11 = -C$

i) $81 = \dfrac{9D}{9}$

j) $8 = \dfrac{U}{5}$

k) $63 = 9Y$

l) $8 = -4W$

Problem Solving

Try this word problem.
   Read the problem.

m) Al's backpack could carry 5 books. How many backpacks would Al need to carry 25 books?

1. Set up the equation. Explain your reasoning.
2. Answer the equation using ISOLATE. Show all of your work. What is the answer? Does it make sense, and why?

Student **LESSON # 9**

Abstract II

Describe/Model

a) $T5 = 12$

b) $7 = \dfrac{2M}{3}$

Guided Practice

c) $12 = \dfrac{2X}{5}$

d) $5C = -33$

Independent Practice

e) $3X = 28$

f) $\dfrac{K}{7} = 6$

g) $19 = X3$

h) $64 = 4X$

i) $2Y = -17$

j) $6R = 8$

k) $5 = \dfrac{2N}{3}$

l) $\dfrac{4P}{6} = 3$

Problem Solving

m) Jose had 20 pencils and gave some away. He had 3 left. How many did he give away? Set up the equation and solve.

n) There are 11 players per team and many teams. If there are 33 players, how many teams are there? Set up the equation and solve.

Teaching **LESSON # 9**

Abstract II

Describe/Model

Purpose: Solving equations using hands-on and pictorial methods taught the procedures for solving equations. Now we are going to go a little faster. Instead of using concrete and pictorial ways to solve for the variable, we are going to write out the numbers and solve the equations abstractly. Be careful, as some of the answers in this section are in the form of fractions.

Note: If the students struggle with fractions, please examine Computation of Fractions (Witzel & Riccomini, 2008) as another possible intervention.

Let's get started.

Describe/Model

9a) Let's set up the problem as it is written: T5 = 12.

I—I want to solve for T, so I need to find out what is in 1 T.

S—There are no other calculations on the same side as T, so I will divide each side of the equation by 5.

O—I draw a divisor line and 5 on both sides.

L—Let's calculate.

A—Answer the unknown side: 5 divided by 5 is 1. So I have 1T.

T—Total the other side: 12 divided by 5 leaves 2 full groups of 5 and 2 left over. This equates to $2\frac{2}{5}$.

E—The answer is 1T = $2\frac{2}{5}$.

9b) Let's set up the problem as it is written: $7 = \dfrac{2M}{3}$.

I—I want to solve for M, so I need to find out what is in 1 M.

S—There is no other number aside from the coefficient on the same side as M, so I will divide each side of the equation by 2 and multiply both sides by 3.

O—I draw a divisor line with 3 in the numerator and 2 in the denominator on both sides.

L—Let's calculate.

A—Answer the unknown side: 2 divided by 2 is 1, and 3 divided by 3 is 1. I am left with 1M.

T—Total the other side: 3 times 7 is 21. Next, 21 divided by 2 is 10 with 1 left over.

E—The answer is 1M = 10 ½.

Guided Practice

In this section, I will go through the steps for the first one and you will complete it with me step-by-step. For the last one, you will work at least one step ahead of me.

Go through each step by asking what to do and doing it as close to simultaneously with the students as possible.

9c) $12 = \dfrac{2X}{5}$

I—I want to solve for what variable?

S—What is the coefficient, and what should I do next?

O—What do I place on both sides?

L—Let's calculate.

A—Answer the unknown side.

T—Total the other side.

E—The answer is what? Yes, 1X = 30.

Now it is your turn to work one step ahead of me.

For d), go through ISOLATE one step at a time, having students perform the step first. Then, check their work and go accordingly.

9d) 5C = −33

Independent Practice

Now it is your turn. Complete these eight problems on your own pictorially without help. I will be walking around to assess how you are doing but not necessarily to help.

e) 3X = 28

f) $\dfrac{K}{7} = 6$

g) 19 = X3

h) 64 = 4X

i) 2Y = −17

j) 6R = 8

k) $5 = \dfrac{2N}{3}$

l) $\dfrac{4P}{6} = 3$

Problem Solving

Try these word problems.
    Read the problem.

m) Jose had 20 pencils and gave some away. He had 3 left. How many did he give away?

    1. Set up the equation. Explain your reasoning.
    2. Answer the equation using ISOLATE. Show all of your work. What is the answer? Does it make sense, and why?

    Read the problem.

n) There are 11 players per team and many teams. If there are 33 players, how many teams are there?

    1. Set up the equation. Explain your reasoning.
    2. Answer the equation using ISOLATE. Show all of your work. What is the answer? Does it make sense, and why?

Student   **LESSON # 10**

Fluency/Work Fast

a) $3X = -27$

b) $\dfrac{X}{2} = 5$

c) $18 = X3$

d) $24 = 6X$

e) $-2Y = 18$

f) $3Y = 9$

g) $5 = \dfrac{1Y}{3}$

h) $\dfrac{2Y}{5} = 3$

i) $5N = -20$

j) $12 = 3N$

k) $8 = \dfrac{N}{4}$

l) $1 = -8N$

m) $6 = \dfrac{3P}{4}$

n) $2 = \dfrac{P}{5}$

o) $81 = -9P$

p) $16 = -8P$

Teaching **LESSON # 10**

Fluency/Work Fast

Now that you have shown that you know how to solve one-step equations, let's see how many accurate answers you can give in a 2-minute timed quiz. The problems in this quiz are all different, so read each problem carefully. We will start with this one. *(Point to any problem on the sheet.)* Once you give an answer, do not stop; go to the next question on the sheet to the right, or return to the next line below. Answer every question. If you skip a question, that counts as incorrect. If you happen to come to the last problem on the sheet, continue with the problem at the top of the paper and do not stop. *(Run finger across and down the lines of problems to read like a paragraph.)* I will stop you 2 minutes after I say go.

Ready? Go.

(Total student correct and incorrect answers during the 2 minutes on a separate sheet of paper. Upon completion, tell the students what you tallied and have each student graph his or her performance. You may want to talk about the growth of the students' performance between lessons.)

Student LESSON # 11

Concrete/Hands-on (Two-Step Equations)

Describe/Model

a) $1N + 5 = 8$ b) $4 = X - 5$

c) $2N + 3 = 7$ d) $8 = 0 + 3Y$

Guided Practice

e) $X - 3 = 5$ f) $7 + 2N = 8$

g) $11 = 3 + 4Y$ h) $9 = 3X + 3$

Independent Practice

i) $X - 4 = 2$ j) $8 = 2Y + 1$

k) $8 = 2Y + 4$ l) $1 = 3N - 5$

Problem Solving

m) A cake has 18 pieces. The pieces were divided among a few people. In the end (=), each person received 3 pieces of cake, how many people were there? Set up the equation and solve for the variable.

n) The shop owner earned $15. She gives you some for helping her (+X). You see (=) she kept $2. How much money does she give you? Set up the equation and solve for the variable.

Teaching **LESSON # 11**

Concrete/Hands-on (Two-Step Equations)

Purpose: When we simplified expressions, we tried to find out what was essential about each expression. When we solved for the one-step equations, we did something similar in that we found out what was essential and then computed to find the unknown. Now the equations grow a bit longer and more complex. This is okay because we will follow the same steps as we did in the last few lessons.

Relevance: As math becomes more complex you will see that it is more difficult to find your answer. This makes sense. As we grow older, problems in life become more complex. You will take out a loan one day and have to figure out how best you can pay it off so that you do not go bankrupt and people take back whatever it is that you bought. So, if you want to buy a car, a home, or even a computer through a loan, these are the basic forms of equations you will need to know. If you are ever to run a business, these are types of problems that you need to know. The good news is that you already have a good idea as to how to answer them. This is another step toward complex mathematics.

Let's get started.

Describe/Model

11a) Let's set up the problem as it is written: 1N + 5 = 8.

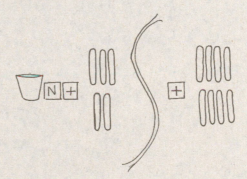

I—I want to solve for N, so I need to find out what is in 1 cup, the coefficient, of N.

S—On the same side as 1N, I have a +5. That means that first I will have to subtract 5 from both sides and then divide each side of the equation by 1 cup.

O—I place a −5, a divisor line, and 1 cup on both sides

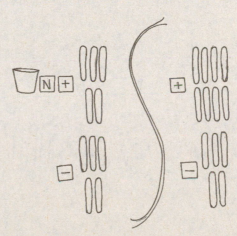

L—Let's calculate.

A—Answer the unknown side: I have +5 sticks −5 sticks. They are opposite signs, so remove an equal number of sticks from both numbers. I am left with zero, or nothing. Next, I divide 1 cup by 1. 1 divided by 1 is 1.

T—Total the other side: 8 sticks −5 sticks. They are opposite, so I remove an equal number of sticks from each group. I am left with +3 sticks.

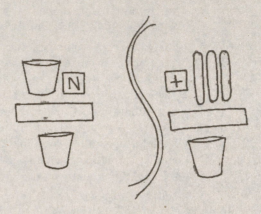

Next, I divide the 3 sticks in 1 cup. The answer is 1 cup of 3 sticks, or 3 sticks per cup.

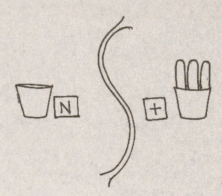

E—The answer is 1N = 3

11b) Let's set up the problem as it is written: 4 = X − 5.

I—I want to solve for X, so I need to find out what is in 1 cup, the coefficient, of X.

S—Since there is a −5 on the same side of X, I want to get rid of that. To do so, I add 5 sticks to each side. Next, I will divide each side of the equation by the coefficient, 1 cup.

O—First, I add 5 sticks to both sides, and then I place a divisor line and 4 cups on both sides.

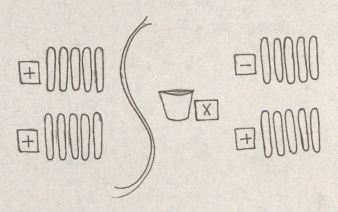

L—Let's calculate.

A—Answer the unknown side: −5 sticks +5 sticks work in opposite directions on a number line. So, I will pull an equal amount from each group. The answer is zero. Next, I divide 1 cup by 1 cup, and the answer is 1.

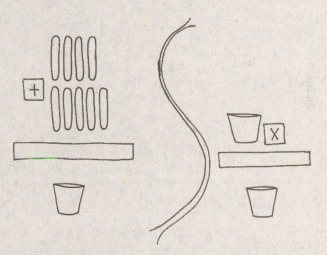

T—Total the other side: 4 sticks plus 5 sticks equals 9 sticks. I bring them together.

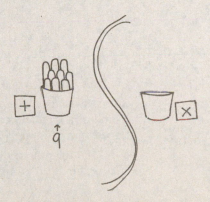

Then I divide the 9 sticks into 1 cup. It is a tight fit, but I am left with 9 sticks per cup of X.

E—The answer is 9 = 1X, or 1X = 9.

11c) Let's set up the problem as it is written: 2N + 3 = 7.

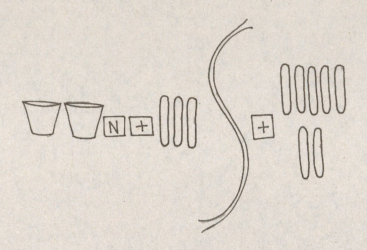

I—I want to solve for N, so I need to find out what is in 1 cup of N.

S—Since there is a +3 on the same side as the 2N, it is easier to move that first. So I will need to add −3 to each side. Then I will divide each side by the coefficient of 2, in this case, 2 cups.

O—I place −3 sticks, a divisor line, and 2 cups on both sides.

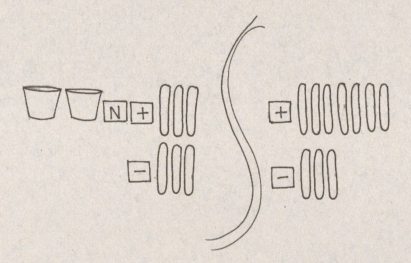

L—Let's calculate.

A—Answer the unknown side: +3 sticks −3 sticks means I pull an equal number from both. I am left with no sticks. Then I divide 2 cups by 2 cups, which is 1. I have 1 cup of N remaining.

T—Total the other side: 7 sticks −3 sticks means that I pull an equal number of sticks from both groups. I am left with 4 sticks.

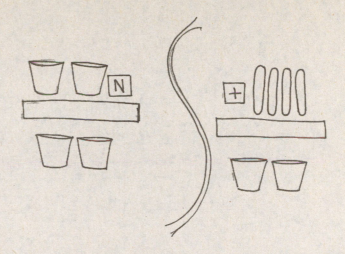

Then I divide those 4 sticks into 2 cups.

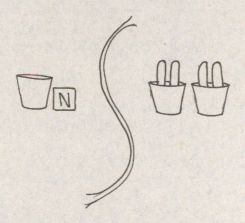

E—The answer is 2 sticks per cup, or 1N = 2.

11d) Let's set up the problem as it is written: 8 = 0 + 3Y.

I—I want to solve for Y, so I need to find out what is in 1 cup of Y.

S—Since there is a zero to be added on the same side of 3Y, I do not need to anything with it. Next, I focus on the coefficient. I will divide each side by 3 cups.

O—I place a divisor line and 3 cups on both sides.

L—Let's calculate.

A—Answer the unknown side: 3 divided by 3 is 1. Thus, I have 1Y.

T—Total the other side; 8 sticks divided into 3 cups equally leaves me 2 sticks per cup and 2 left over.

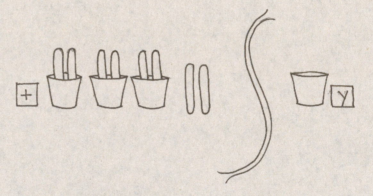

E—The answer is 2 and 2 sticks that could not break into 3 cups: 2⅔.

If you need, I can break the remaining sticks into 3 pieces each to show that 2 and 2/3 sticks go equally into 3 cups.

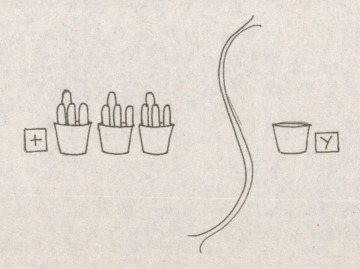

Guided Practice

In this section, I will go through the steps for the first two and you will complete them with me step-by-step. By the last two, you will work at least one step ahead of me.

Go through each step by asking what to do and doing it as close to simultaneously with the students as possible.

11e) $X - 3 = 5$

I—I want to solve for what variable?

S—Before I can use the coefficient, I must remove the -3. To do that, I add 3 to both sides of the equation. *Place +3 sticks on both sides.* Next, I work with the coefficient, 1. I will divide each side by 1 cup. *Place the cups and divisors on both sides of the equation.*

O—What do I place on both sides?

L—Let's calculate.

A—Answer the unknown side: $-3 + 3$ equals 0, so I remove those pieces. 1 divided by 1 is 1. Thus, I have 1X.

T—Total the other side: 5 sticks +3 sticks is 8 sticks. Next, I divide the 8 sticks into 1 cup.

E—The answer is what? Yes, 1X = 8 sticks per cup, or 8.

11f) $7 + 2N = 8$

I—I want to solve for what variable?

S—Before I can use the coefficient, I must remove the 7. To do that, I subtract 7 from both sides of the equation. *Place −7 sticks on both sides.* Next, I work with the coefficient, 2. I will divide each side by 2 cups. *Place the cups and divisors on both sides of the equation.*

O—What do I place on both sides?

L—Let's calculate.

A—Answer the unknown side: $7 - 7$ sticks equals 0, so I remove those pieces. 2 divided by 2 is 1. Thus, I have 1N.

T—Total the other side: 8 sticks −7 sticks is 1 stick remaining. Next, I divide the 1 stick by 2 cups.

E—The answer is what? Yes, 1N = ½ stick per cup, or ½.

Now it is your turn to work one step ahead of me.

For g) and h), go through ISOLATE one step at a time, having students perform the step first. Then, check their work and go accordingly.

g) $11 = 3 + 4Y$

h) $9 = 3X + 3$

Independent Practice

Now it is your turn. Complete these four problems on your own concretely. I will be walking around to assess how you are doing but not necessarily to help.

i) $X - 4 = 2$ j) $8 = 2Y + 1$

k) $8 = 2Y + 4$ l) $1 = 3N - 5$

Problem Solving

Let's try a couple of these together.
   Read the problem.

m) A cake has 18 pieces. The pieces were divided among a few people. In the end (=), each person received 3 pieces of cake. How many people were there? Set up the equation and solve for the variable.

1. Set up the equation concretely. Explain your reasoning.
2. Answer the equation. Go through the steps to ISOLATE concretely. Does it make sense, and why?

   Read the problem.

n) The shop owner earned $15. She gives you some for helping her (+X). You see (=) she kept $2. How much money does she give you? Set up the equation and solve for the variable.

1. Set up the equation concretely. Explain your reasoning.
2. Answer the equation. Go through the steps to ISOLATE concretely. Does it make sense, and why?

Student **LESSON # 12**

Representational/Pictures (Two-Step Equations)

Describe/Model

a) $10 - N = 3$

b) $12 = -5 + 2X$

c) $\dfrac{Y}{5} + 1 = 5$

d) $6 = \dfrac{12}{Y}$

Guided Practice

e) $-4 = 8 - 4C$

f) $5W - 2 = 10$

g) $5 = \dfrac{25}{Y}$

h) $\dfrac{2M}{3} = 4$

Independent Practice

i) $9 = -2Y + 3$

j) $6 - 4X = -2$

k) $\dfrac{14}{W} = 2$

l) $\dfrac{2N}{3} = 5$

Problem Solving

m) You pull out $20 to pay for your haircut. You don't know how much the haircut costs. After you hand the money over (=), the barber hands you $7 change. How much did the haircut cost?

n) Mr. W. had to divide 8 books among some students (N). Each student had 2 books. How many students were there? Set up the equation and solve.

Teaching **LESSON # 12**

Representational/Pictures (Two-Step Equations)

Now we will draw pictures of similar problems to the ones we answered with the hands-on materials. Follow along with how I do this. This notation will allow you to think through some of these problems on tests and at home. This problems has some extra twists, like the unknown in the denominator or fractional and negative coefficients.

Note: This section has integers within it as both addends and coefficients. If integers are difficult for students, please review the Computation of Integers intervention (Riccomini & Witzel, 2009).

Let's get started.

Describe/Model

12a) Let's set up the problem as it is written: $10 - N = 3$.

I—I want to solve for N, so I need to find out what is in 1 group, the coefficient, of N.

S—On the same side as 1N, I have a +10. That means that first I will have to subtract 10 from both sides and then divide each side of the equation by 1 group and a negative.

O—I draw a −10, a divisor line, and 1 group and a negative sign on both sides.

L—Let's calculate.

A—Answer the unknown side: I have +10 tallies −10 tallies. They are opposite signs so I cross out an equal number of tallies from both numbers. I am left with no tallies: zero. Next, I divide by a negative and 1 group: 1 divided by 1 is 1. Negative divided by a negative is a positive. I am left with +1N.

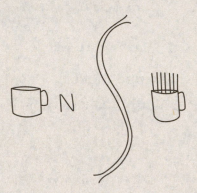

T—Total the other side: 3 tallies −10 tallies. They are opposite, so I cross out an equal number of tallies from each group. I am left with a −7 tallies.

Next, I divide the 7 tallies into 1 group. The answer is 1 group of 7 tallies. Finally, I divide the negative sign by a negative sign. A negative divided by a negative is a positive.

E—The answer is 1N = 7.

12b) Let's set up the problem as it is written: 12 = −5 + 2X.

I—I want to solve for X, so I need to find out what is in 1 group of X.

S—Since there is a −5 on the same side of X, I want to get rid of that. To do so, I add 5 tallies to each side. Next, I will divide each side of the equation by the coefficient, 2 groups.

O—First, I add 5 tallies to both sides, and then I draw a divisor line and 2 groups to both sides.

L—Let's calculate.

A—Answer the unknown side: −5 tallies +5 tallies work in opposite directions on a number line. So, I will cross out an equal number from each group. The answer is zero. Next, I divide 2 groups by 2 groups, and the answer is 1. I circle both groups to show this.

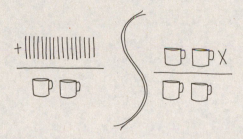

T—Total the other side: 12 tallies plus 5 tallies equals 17 tallies.

Then, I divide the 17 tallies into 2 groups. In this case, I draw 8 tallies in each group with 1 tally left over.

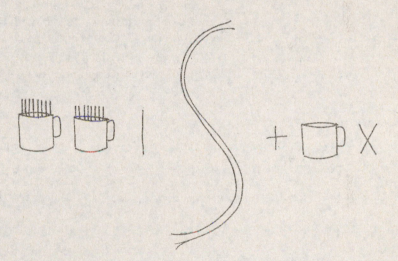

E—The answer is 8 tallies per group and 1 tally that needs to go into 2 groups: 8½ tallies per group. 1X = 8½.

12c) Let's set up the problem as it is written: Y/5 + 1 = 5. I draw a 1/5 for the coefficient of Y.

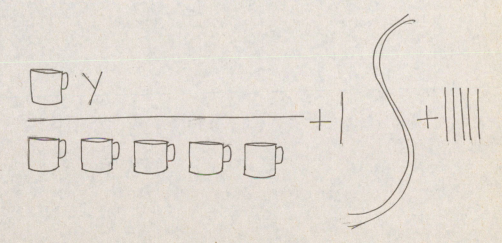

I—I want to solve for Y, so I need to find out what is in 1 group of Y.

S—Since there is a +1 on the same side as the 1/5 Y, it is easier to move that first. So I draw a −1 on each side. Then I will multiply each side by 5 groups and divide each side by 1.

O—I draw −1, 5 groups, a divisor line, and 1 group on both sides.

L—Let's calculate.

A—Answer the unknown side: +1 tallies −1 tally means I cross out an equal number of both groups. I am left with no tallies. Then I multiply by 5 and divide by 1. 5 divided by 5 is 1, and 1 divided by 1 is 1. Thus, I have 1Y.

T—Total the other side: 5 tallies −1 tally is 4 tallies. Then, I multiply the 4 tallies in 5 different groups. So, I draw 4 tallies in 5 groups. I now have 20 tallies.

Next, I divide those 20 tallies into one group. That gives me 20 tallies per group.

E—The answer is Y = 20.

12d) Let's set up the problem as it is written: 6 = 12/Y. I place 1 group next to the Y, which is in the denominator in this problem. The 1 is not the coefficient in this case, since there is a whole number besides and under the Y.

TEACHING LESSON # 12

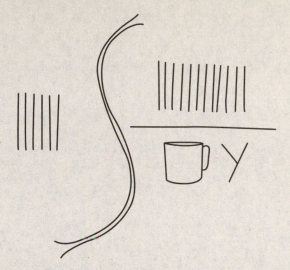

I—I want to solve for Y, so I need to find out what is in 1 group of Y.

S—Since there is no other number on the same side of the Y, I will immediately work with the coefficient. I will multiply both sides by 1 group of Y.

O—I place a 1 group and a Y on both sides

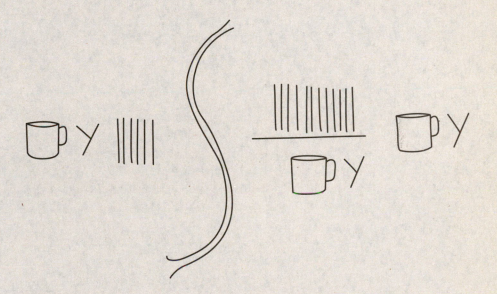

L—Let's calculate.

A—Answer the unknown side: 1Y divided 1Y is 1. I can cross both groups out.

T—Total the other side: 6 tallies times 1 group of Y is 1 cup of 6 tallies of Y.

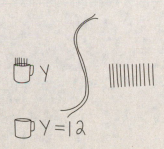

E—I am now left with 6Y = 12.

We are not done yet. Let's start anew.

12d) Let's set up the problem as it is written: 6Y = 12.

I—I want to solve for Y, so I need to find out what is in 1 group of Y.

S—Since there is no other number on the same side of the Y, I will immediately work with the coefficient. I will divide both sides by 6 groups.

O—I place a divisor and 6 groups on both sides.

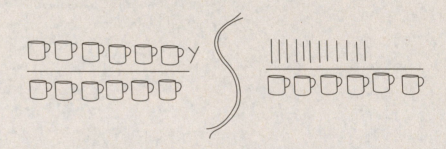

L—Let's calculate.

A—Answer the unknown side: 6 divided by 6 is 1. I cross them out to indicate this. I am left with 1Y.

T—Total the other side: 12 tallies into 6 groups comes out to 2 tallies per group.

E—I am now left with 1Y = 2.

Are we done now? Yes.

Let's talk about what happened in this complex problem.

Where was the unknown? Yes, the denominator.

What did we have to do? We multiplied both sides by the denominator.

But we were not done. What else did we have to do? Yes, we have to then divide both sides by the new coefficient.

It isn't too different from the other problems, but you will have to check to see that you have 1 group in your answer.

How else could we have answered this problem?

$6 = 12/Y$

To bring Y into the numerator and move the number on the other side of the problem, we could do two calculations at the same time.

$6Y/6 = 12Y/Y6$

Each side of the equation was multiplied by Y and divided by 6.

After we calculate this we are left with $1Y = 2$.

Guided Practice

In this section, I will go through the steps for the first two and you will complete them with me step-by-step. By the last two, you will work at least one step ahead of me.

Go through each step by asking what to do and doing it as close to simultaneously with them as possible.

12e) $-4 = 8 - 4C$

I—I want to solve for what variable?

S—Before I can use the coefficient, I must remove the 8. To do that, I subtract 8 from both sides of the equation. *Draw −8 tallies on both sides.* Next, I work with the coefficient, −4. I will divide each side by − and 4 groups. *Draw the negative, groups, and divisors on both sides of the equation.*

O—What do I place on both sides? *Make certain the equations are balanced.*

L—Let's calculate.

A—Answer the unknown side. 8 − 8 equals 0 so I cross out those pieces. −4 divided by −4 is 1. Thus, I have 1C.

T—Total the other side: −4 tallies −8 tallies is −12 tallies. Next, I divide the −12 tallies among 4 groups with another negative remaining. Remember, negative divided by a negative is a positive.

E—The answer is what? Yes, $1C = -3$ tallies per group, or −3.

12f) $5W - 2 = 10$

I—I want to solve for what variable?

S—Before I can use the coefficient, I must remove the −2. To do that, I add 2 to both sides of the equation. *Draw +2 tallies on both sides.* Next, I work with the coefficient, 5. I will divide each side by 5 groups. *Draw the groups and divisors on both sides of the equation.*

O—What do I place on both sides? *Make certain the equations are balanced.*

L—Let's calculate.

A—Answer the unknown side: −2 + 2 equals 0, so I cross out those pieces. 5 divided by 5 is 1. Thus, I have 1W.

T—Total the other side: 10 + 2 tallies is 12 tallies. Next, I divide the 12 tallies among 5 groups.

E—The answer is what? Yes, $1W = 2\frac{2}{5}$.

Now it is your turn to work one step ahead of me.

For g) and h), go through ISOLATE one step at a time, having students perform the step first. Then, check their work and go accordingly.

g) $5 = \dfrac{25}{Y}$ h) $\dfrac{2M}{3} = 4$

Independent Practice

Now it is your turn. Complete these four problems on your own concretely. I will be walking around to assess how you are doing but not necessarily to help.

i) $9 = -2Y + 3$

j) $6 - 4X = -2$

k) $\dfrac{14}{W} = 2$

l) $\dfrac{2N}{3} = 5$

Problem Solving

Let's try a couple of these together.
Read the problem.

m) You pull out $20 to pay for your haircut. You don't know how much the haircut costs. After you hand the money over (=), the barber hands you $7 change. How much did the haircut cost?

1. Set up the equation pictorially. Explain your reasoning.
2. Answer the equation. Go through the steps to ISOLATE pictorially. Does it make sense, and why?

Read the problem.

n) Mr. W. had to divide 8 books among some students (N). Each student had 2 books. How many students were there?

1. Set up the equation pictorially. Explain your reasoning.
2. Answer the equation. Go through the steps to ISOLATE pictorially. Does it make sense, and why?

Student **LESSON # 13**

Abstract

Describe/Model

a) $\dfrac{72}{P} = 8$

b) $8 = 14 - H2$

Guided Practice

c) $\dfrac{36}{M} = 9$

d) $9 = -7 - \dfrac{1C}{3}$

Independent Practice

e) $-13 - X = 13$

f) $-2X + 13 = -7$

g) $8 = \dfrac{32}{N}$

h) $\dfrac{2R}{4} = 6$

i) $19 = -Y + 18$

j) $9 = \dfrac{54}{Y}$

k) $\dfrac{44}{K} = 11$

l) $2 + \dfrac{1P}{2} = 22$

Problem Solving

m) 90 of Suzie's closest friends came to her birthday party. She divides them into several teams to play football. If each team has 9 people, how many teams are there? Set up the equation and solve.

n) Last year it rained an unknown amount. It rained 10 inches less this year. This year it rained 28 inches. How many inches did it rain last year? Set the equation and solve.

Teaching LESSON # 13

Abstract

Describe/Model

Purpose: Solving equations using hands-on and pictorial methods taught us the procedures for solving multistep equations. Now we are going to go a little faster. Instead of using concrete and pictorial ways to solve for the variable, we are going to write out the numbers and solve the equations abstractly.

Let's get started.

Describe/Model

13a) Let's set up the problem as it is written: $72/P = 8$.

I—I want to solve for P, so I need to find out what is in 1 P. We went through a few problems like this in the previous lesson, so let's remember what we did to solve for 1P.

S—Since 1P is in the denominator and I want it in the numerator, I will multiply both sides by 1P.

O—I write 1P on both sides.

L—Let's calculate.

A—Answer the unknown side. Let's go from the original side of P: 1P divided by 1P is 1. Now I have $72 = 8P$.

We are not done yet, so I will go back to P.

S—I want to know what is in 1 P, so I divide each side by the coefficient, 8.

O—I draw a divisor and 8 on both sides.

L—I calculate.

A—8P divided by 8 is 1P.

T—Total the other side: 72 divided by 8 is 9.

E—The answer is $1P = 9$.

13b) Let's set up the problem as it is written: $8 = 14 - H2$.

I—I want to solve for H, so I need to find out what is in 1 H.

S—I first want to move the 14, so I subtract 14 from both sides. Next, I divide the coefficient, − and 2, from both sides.

O—Both sides have a −14 and are divided by −2.

L—Let's calculate.

A—Answer the unknown side: $14 - 14$ is 0. −H2 divided by −2 is 1H. I am left with 1H.

T—Total the other side: $8 - 14$ is −6. Next, −6 divided by −2 is 3.

E—The answer is $1H = 3$.

Guided Practice

In this section, I will go through the steps for the first one and you will complete it with me step-by-step. For the last one, you will work at least one step ahead of me.

Go through each step by asking what to do and doing it as close to simultaneously with the students as possible.

13c) $36/M = 9$

    I—I want to solve for what variable?

    S—What is the coefficient, and what should I do next? Yes, multiply both sides by M.

    O—What do I place on both sides?

    L—Let's calculate.

    A—Answer the unknown side: 36M/M is 36.

    T—Total the other side: 9M.

    Start over:

    S—Divide both sides by 9.

    O—Divisor and 9.

    L—Let's calculate.

    A—9M/9 is 1M.

    T—36/9 = 4.

    E—The answer is what? Yes, 1M = 4.

    Now it is your turn to work one step ahead of me.

    For d), go through ISOLATE one step at a time, having students perform the step first. Then, check their work and go accordingly.

d) $9 = -7 - 1C/3$

Independent Practice

Now it is your turn. Complete these eight problems on your own pictorially without help. I will be walking around to assess how you are doing but not necessarily to help.

e) $-13 - X = 13$ f) $-2X + 13 = -7$

g) $8 = \dfrac{32}{N}$ h) $\dfrac{2R}{4} = 6$

i) $19 = -Y + 18$ j) $9 = \dfrac{54}{Y}$

k) $\dfrac{44}{K} = 11$ l) $2 + \dfrac{1P}{2} = 22$

Problem Solving

Try this word problem.
  Read the problem.

m) 90 of Suzie's closest friends came to her birthday party. She divides them into several teams to play football. If each team has 9 people, how many teams are there?

  1. Set up the equation. Explain your reasoning.
  2. Answer the equation using ISOLATE. Show all of your work. What is the answer? Does it make sense, and why?

  Read the problem.

n) Last year it rained an unknown amount. It rained 10 inches less this year. This year it rained 28 inches. How many inches did it rain last year?

  1. Set up the equation. Explain your reasoning.
  2. Answer the equation using ISOLATE. Show all of your work. What is the answer? Does it make sense, and why?

Student **LESSON # 14**

Abstract II

Describe/Model

a) $52 = -4A + 32$ b) $\dfrac{48}{X} + 1 = 7$

Guided Practice

c) $\dfrac{2W}{5} = 6$ d) $17 = 14 - H2$

Independent Practice

e) $3 = \dfrac{30}{Y}$ f) $-4J - 8 = 16$

g) $23 = \dfrac{23}{G}$ h) $\dfrac{3Y}{2} = 6$

i) $9 = 2Y + 8$ j) $16 - X = 12$

k) $\dfrac{48}{6} = 8$ l) $2 - \dfrac{N}{6} = 8$

m) $2 = \dfrac{2M}{5}$ n) $19 = -10 - D$

Problem Solving

o) Mrs. Millionaire owned 10 cars and divided them among her daughters. If each daughter ended up with 2 cars, how many daughters were there?

p) Margie was loaned money by her mom, but she forgot how much. In her pocket she found a store receipt that said she spent $10 for a CD and had $10 change. How much did her mother loan her? Set up the equation and solve.

Teaching **LESSON # 14**
Abstract II

Describe/Model

Purpose: Solving equations using hands-on and pictorial methods taught us the procedures for solving multistep equations. Now we are going to go a little faster. Instead of using concrete and pictorial ways to solve for the variable, we are going to write out the numbers and solve the equations abstractly.

Describe/Model

14a) Let's set up the problem as it is written: $52 = -4A + 32.$

I—I want to solve for A, so I need to find out what is in 1 A.

S—I first want to move the 32, so I subtract 32 from both sides. Next, I divide the coefficient, − and 4, from both sides.

O—Both sides have a −32 and are divided by −4.

L—Let's calculate.

A—Answer the unknown side: $32 - 32$ is 0. $-4A$ divided by −4 is 1A. I am left with 1A.

T—Total the other side: $32 - 32$ is 20. Next, 20 divided by −4 is −5.

E—The answer is $1A = -5$.

14b) Let's set up the problem as it is written: $48/X + 1 = 7.$

I—I want to solve for X, so I need to find out what is in 1 X.

S—I first want to move the +1, so I subtract 1 from both sides. Since 1X is in the denominator and I want it in the numerator, I will multiply both sides by 1X.

O—I write −1 and 1X on both sides.

L—Let's calculate.

A—Answer the unknown side. Let's go from the original side of X: $1 - 1$ is 0. $48/X$ is 48.

T—Now I have $7 + 1 = 8$. 8 times 1X is 8X.

We now have $48 = 8X$.

We are not done yet, so I will go back to S.

S—I want to know what is in 1 X, so I divide each side by the coefficient, 8.

O—I draw a divisor and 8 on both sides.

L—I calculate.

A—8X divided by 8 is 1X.

T—Total the other side: 48 divided by 8 is 6.

E—The answer is $1X = 8$.

Guided Practice

In this section, I will go through the steps for the first one and you will complete it with me step-by-step. For the last one, you will work at least one step ahead of me.

Go through each step by asking what to do and doing it as close to simultaneously with the students as possible.

14c) $2W/5 = 6$

I—I want to solve for what variable?

S—What is the coefficient, and what should I do next? Yes, multiply both sides by 5 and divide both sides by 2.

O—What do I place on both sides? *Show your work.*

L—Let's calculate.

A—Answer the unknown side: 2 divided by 2 is one1, and 5 divided by 5 is 1. I am left with 1W.

T—Total the other side: 6 times 5 is 30. 30 divided by 2 is 15.

E—The answer is what? Yes, 1W = 15.

Now it is your turn to work one step ahead of me.

For d), go through ISOLATE one step at a time, having students perform the step first. Then, check their work and go accordingly.

d) $-4J - 8 = 16$

Independent Practice

Now it is your turn. Complete these eight problems on your own pictorially without help. I will be walking around to assess how you are doing but not necessarily to help.

e) $3 = \dfrac{30}{Y}$ f) $-4J - 8 = 16$

g) $23 = \dfrac{23}{G}$ h) $\dfrac{3Y}{2} = 6$

i) $9 = 2Y + 8$ j) $16 - X = 12$

k) $\dfrac{48}{6} = 8$ l) $2 - \dfrac{N}{6} = 8$

m) $2 = \dfrac{2M}{5}$ n) $19 = -10 - D$

Problem Solving

Try this word problem.
Read the problem.

o) Mrs. Millionaire owned 10 cars and divided them among her daughters. If each daughter ended up with 2 cars, how many daughters were there?

1. Set up the equation. Explain your reasoning.
2. Answer the equation using ISOLATE. Show all of your work. What is the answer? Does it make sense, and why?

Read the problem.

p) Margie was loaned money by her mom, but she forgot how much. In her pocket she found a store receipt that said she spent $10 for a CD and had $10 change. How much did her mother loan her?

1. Set up the equation. Explain your reasoning.
2. Answer the equation using ISOLATE. Show all of your work. What is the answer? Does it make sense, and why?

Student **LESSON # 15**

Level 1: Fluency/Work Fast

a) $5 = X - 8$

b) $3X = 27$

c) $4 + X = 5$

d) $\dfrac{X}{8} = 6$

e) $16 = X + 7$

f) $25 = 5X$

g) $Y - 11 = 2$

h) $9 = 3Y$

i) $\dfrac{Y}{2} = 6$

j) $Y - 6 = 13$

k) $-3 = \dfrac{Y}{9}$

l) $14 = 2 + Y$

m) $13 = W - 14$

n) $64 = 4W$

o) $\dfrac{W}{6} = 7$

p) $W - 18 = 8$

q) $54 = 14 + W$

r) $\dfrac{W}{7} = 6$

s) $N + 8 = 26$

t) $63 = 9N$

u) $19 = N - 3$

v) $-2 + N = 17$

w) $7 = \dfrac{N}{7}$

x) $23 + N = 1$

y) $\dfrac{P}{10} = 3$

z) $16 = 4P$

aa) $16 = P - 7$

bb) $11 = 22 + P$

cc) $8 = \dfrac{P}{4}$

dd) $P5 = 25$

Teaching **LESSON # 15**

Step1: Fluency/Work Fast

Now that you have shown that you know how to solve multistep equations, let's see how many accurate answers you can give in a 2-minute timed quiz. The problems in this quiz are all different, so read each problem carefully. We will start with this one. *(Point to any problem on the sheet.)* Once you give an answer, do not stop; go to the next question on the sheet to the right, or return to the next line below. Answer every question. If you skip a question, that counts as incorrect. If you happen to come to the last problem on the sheet, continue with the problem at the top of the paper and do not stop. *(Run finger across and down the lines of problems to read like a paragraph.)* I will stop you 2 minutes after I say go.

Ready? Go.

(Total student correct and incorrect answers during the 2 minutes on a separate sheet of paper. Upon completion, tell the students what you tallied and have each student graph his or her performance. You may want to talk about the growth of the students' performance between lessons.)

Student   **LESSON # 15**

Level 2: Fluency/Work Fast

a) $3 = -Y + 16$ b) $-2Y - 10 = 2$ c) $\dfrac{39}{Y} = 13$

d) $\dfrac{21}{Y} = 3$ e) $11 - 3Y = 15$ f) $\dfrac{-Y}{2} - 2 = 16$

g) $4 = \dfrac{2M}{5}$ h) $\dfrac{27}{M} = 3$ i) $9 = -M + 7$

j) $-17 - 7M = 17$ k) $\dfrac{24}{M} = 6$ l) $\dfrac{M}{3} = 7$

m) $4 = \dfrac{2W}{5}$ n) $9 = -5W + 8$ o) $21 - W = 21$

p) $8 = \dfrac{2W}{3}$ q) $\dfrac{45}{W} = 5$ r) $19 = -3W + 18$

s) $16 - 4X = 12$ t) $\dfrac{4X}{5} = 7$ u) $2 = \dfrac{2X}{3}$

v) $-X - 8 = 16$ w) $5X + 13 = -17$ x) $7 = \dfrac{42}{X}$

y) $\dfrac{3U}{4} = 11$ z) $-2 = 13 - 3U$ aa) $\dfrac{54}{U} = 6$

Teaching **LESSON # 15**

Step 2: Fluency/Work Fast

Note: This step has more multistep problems with fractional answers.

Now that you have shown that you know how to solve multistep equations, let's see how many accurate answers you can give in a 2-minute timed quiz. The problems in this quiz are all different, so read each problem carefully. We will start with this one. *(Point to any problem on the sheet.)* Once you give an answer, do not stop; go to the next question on the sheet to the right, or return to the next line below. Answer every question. If you skip a question, that counts as incorrect. If you happen to come to the last problem on the sheet, continue with the problem at the top of the paper and do not stop. *(Run finger across and down the lines of problems to read like a paragraph.)* I will stop you 2 minutes after I say go.

Ready? Go.

(Total student correct and incorrect answers during the 2 minutes on a separate sheet of paper. Upon completion, tell the students what you tallied and have each student graph his or her performance. You may want to talk about the growth of the students' performance between lessons.)

Student   **LESSON # 16**

Concrete/Hands-on: Solving for a Variable When Like Variables Are on the Same Side

Describe/Model

a) $-N + 2N = 8$ b) $9 = -X - X + 5$

c) $10 + 5 = 2X - X + X$ d) $2Y + 1Y = 3$

Guided Practice

e) $5 = -X - 3$ f) $2N + 3 - N = 8$

g) $12 = 4Y - Y + 1Y$ h) $9 = N + 2N$

Independent Practice

i) $7 = -3Y + 2Y$ j) $-X - X - X = 9$

k) $8 = 2N - N + N$ l) $Y + 3Y = 16$

Problem Solving

m) 1 employee's (E) salary must be added (+) to another 3 employees' (3E) salaries. Their total (=) salaries are $12 (for 12,000). How much does each employee earn? Set up the equation and solve.

n) 3 batteries (3B) are added to the 1 battery (1B) in Jan's game controller. The total voltage of the batteries is (=) 16 volts. What is the voltage of each battery? Set up and solve the equation.

Teaching **LESSON # 16**

Concrete/Hands-on: Solving for a Variable When Like Variables Are on the Same Side

Note: There are fractions as answers in this section. If fractions are another difficult step, please review the Intervention Series on Fractions (Witzel & Riccomini, 2009).

Purpose: When we simplified expressions, we tried to find out what was essential about each expression. When we solved for the one- and two-step equations, we did something similar in that we found out what was essential and then computed to find the unknown. Now we will need to simplify the expressions first before we solve for the unknown. The steps to ISOLATE work here as well, but we will add a simplified step in the S step (setting up calculations) before dividing by the coefficient.

Relevance: As math becomes more complex you will see that it is more difficult to find your answer. This makes sense. As we grow older, problems in life become more complex. At times what you are trying to solve for is not easy to determine. We will work on first learning what we are solving for and then go through our calculations to solve for the unknown.

Let's get started.

Describe/Model

16a) Let's set up the problem as it is written: $-N + 2N = 8$.

I—I want to solve for N, so I need to find out what is in 1 cup, the coefficient, of N.

S—I have more than 1 set of N, so I will have to simplify the coefficient of N: $-1N + 2N$. I remove an equal number of cups from the 2 sets and am left with $+1N$. Since I have no other calculations to make on the unknown side of the equation, I must divide both sides by the coefficient.

O—I place a divisor line and 1 cup on both sides.

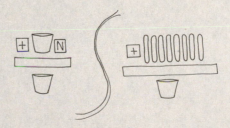

L—Let's calculate.

A—Answer the unknown side. I divide one cup by one: 1 divided by 1 is 1.

T—Total the other side: 8 sticks divided into 1 cup is 8 sticks per cup.

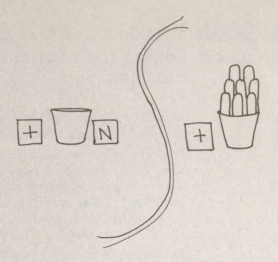

E—The answer is 1N = 8.

16b) Let's set up the problem as it is written: 9 = −X − X + 5.

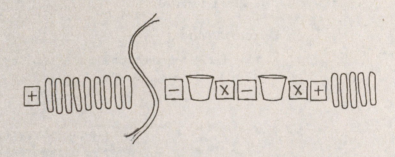

I—I want to solve for X, so I need to find out what is in 1 cup, the coefficient, of X.

S—Since there is more than 1 set of X, I need to simplify the coefficient of X: −1X − 1X. Since both have the same sign, I sum the two and find that I have −2 cups of X. Next, I need to move the 5 on the same side of the unknown. To do so, I subtract 5 sticks from each side. Next, I will divide each side of the equation by the coefficient, −2 cups.

O—First I subtract 5 sticks from both sides. Then I place a divisor line, a negative sign, and 2 cups on both sides.

L—Let's calculate.

A—Answer the unknown side: 5 sticks −5 sticks work in opposite directions on a number line. So, I will pull an equal amount from each group. The answer is zero. Next, I divide 2 cups by 2 cups and find the answer is 1. A negative sign divided by a negative sign is a positive sign. I am left with +1X.

T—Total the other side: 9 sticks minus 5 sticks equals 4 sticks.

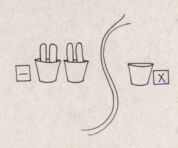

Then I divide the 4 sticks into 2 cups. I am left with 2 sticks per cup.

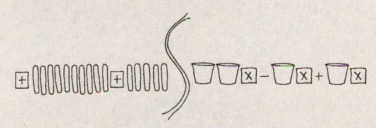

E—The answer is 2 = 1X, or 1X = 2.

16c) Let's set up the problem as it is written: 10 + 5 = 2X − X = X

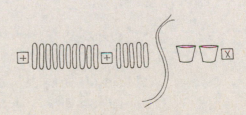

I—I want to solve for X, so I need to find out what is in 1 cup of X.

S—Since there are a few X's on the right side of the equation, I need to simplify the unknown 2X − 1X + 1X. Going from left to right, I start with 2, take away 1, and then add 1. I have 2X remaining. Now that I know the coefficient, I divide both sides by the coefficient: 2.

O—I place a divisor line and 2 cups on both sides.

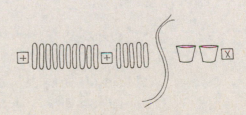

L—Let's calculate.

A—Answer the unknown side: 2 divided by 2 is 1. I have 1 cup of X remaining.

T—Total the other side; 10 sticks +5 sticks equal 15 sticks.

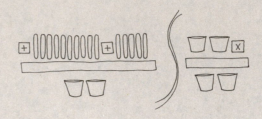

Then I divide those 4 sticks into 2 cups.

Then I divide the 15 sticks into 2 cups. I find that I have 7 sticks per cup with 1 stick left over that didn't divide evenly into 2 cups.

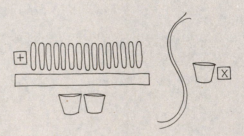

E—The answer is 7½ sticks per cup, or 1X = 7½.

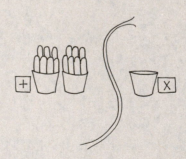

16d) Let's set up the problem as it is written: 2Y + 1Y = 3.

I—I want to solve for Y, so I need to find out what is in 1 cup of Y.

S—Since there are 2 sets of Y on the left side, I will simplify that first: 2Y + 1Y is 3 cups of Y. Now that we know the coefficient, I can more easily solve for Y. I will divide each side by 3 cups.

O—I place a divisor line and 3 cups on both sides.

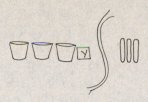

L—Let's calculate.

A—Answer the unknown side: 3 divided by 3 is 1. Thus, I have 1Y.

T—Total the other side: 3 sticks divided into 3 cups equally leaves me with 1 stick per cup.

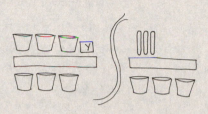

E—The answer is 1 stick per cup, or 1Y = 1.

Guided Practice

In this section, I will go through the steps for the first two and you will complete them with me step-by-step. By the last two, you will work at least one step ahead of me.

Go through each step by asking what to do and doing it as close to simultaneously with the students as possible.

16e) $5 = -X - 3$

I—I want to solve for what variable?

S—Since there is only one set of X on the right side, I do not have to simplify the variable sets first. Now, I must remove the -3. To do that, I add 3 to both sides of the equation. *Place +3 sticks on both sides.* Next, I work with the coefficient, 1. I will divide each side by -1 cup.

O—What do I place on both sides? *Place a negative, a cup, and a divisor line on both sides of the equation.*

L—Let's calculate.

A—Answer the unknown side: $-3 + 3$ equals 0, so I remove those pieces. -1 divided by -1 is 1. Thus, I have 1X.

T—Total the other side: 5 sticks +3 sticks is 8 sticks. Next, I divide the 8 sticks into 1 cup with a negative sign.

E—The answer is what? Yes, 1X = 18 sticks per cup, or 8.

16f) $2N + 3 - N = 8$

I—I want to solve for what variable?

S—Since there are 2 sets of N on the left side, I will simplify that first: $2N - 1N$ is 1 cup of N. Now that we know the coefficient, I can more easily solve for N.

To isolate the N, I must move the +3. To do so, I subtract 3 from both sides. *Place −3 sticks on both sides.* Next, I work with the coefficient, 2. I will divide each side by 1 cup. *Place the cups and divisors on both sides of the equation.*

O—What do I place on both sides? That's right, the objects to show that I subtract 3 and divide by 1.

L—Let's calculate.

A—Answer the unknown side: 7 − 7 sticks equals 0, so I remove those pieces. 2 divided by 2 is 1. Thus, I have 1N.

T—Total the other side: 8 sticks −3 sticks is 5 sticks remaining. Next, I divide the 5 sticks into 1 cup. *Move sticks and cups accordingly.*

E—The answer is what? Yes, 1N = 5 sticks per cup, or 5.

Now it is your turn to work one step ahead of me.

For g) and h), go through ISOLATE one step at a time, having students perform the step first. Then, check their work and go accordingly.

g) $12 = 4Y − Y + 1Y$ h) $9 = N + 2N$

Independent Practice

Now it is your turn. Complete these four problems on your own concretely. I will be walking around to assess how you are doing but not necessarily to help.

i) $7 = −3Y + 2Y$ j) $−X − X − X = 9$

k) $8 = 2N − N + N$ l) $Y + 3Y = 16$

Problem Solving

Let's try a couple of these together.
    Read the problem.

m) 1 employee's (E) salary must be added (+) to another 3 employees' (3E) salaries. Their total (=) salaries are $12 (for 12,000). How much does each employee earn?
  1. Set up the equation and solve.
  2. Answer the equation. Go through the steps to ISOLATE concretely. Does the answer make sense, and why?

   Read the problem.

n) 3 batteries (3B) are added to the 1 battery (1B) in Jan's game controller. The total voltage of the batteries is (=) 16 volts. What is the voltage of each battery?
  1. Set up and solve the equation.
  2. Answer the equation. Go through the steps to ISOLATE concretely. Does the answer make sense, and why?

Student   **LESSON # 17**

Representational/Pictures

Describe/Model

a) $9 + N + 2N = 3$ b) $15 = -4 + 3H - H$

c) $10 + 6 = 2Y - 3Y$ d) $12 = T5 - T + 4$

Guided Practice

e) $-4 = 8 - C(3)$ f) $-2W + W - 2 = 7$

g) $2G + G + G2 = 2 + 3$ h) $2W + W = 13 + 3$

Independent Practice

i) $P4 - 2P = -12 + 8$ j) $5X - X = 11 + 6 - 1$

k) $12 + 2 = 4P + 3P$ l) $12 = 7Y - Y5 + 6$

Problem Solving

m) Chuck brings home 2 paychecks from last week. He adds these to the previous 5 paychecks. He now has made $14 (in thousands). How much is each paycheck? Set up and solve the equation.

n) Marsha cleaned 3 garages on Saturday and 2 garages on Monday. She made $15 on Saturday and $5 on Monday. What is the average amount she earned for each garage cleaned? Set up the equation and solve.

Teaching **LESSON # 17**

Representational/Pictures

Purpose: Now that you have shown you can work through the procedures concretely, today we will work through similar problems pictorially. Again, we will be simplifying the variable expression and then solving for that variable.

Let's get started.

Describe/Model

17a) Let's set up the problem as it is written: $9 + N + 2N = 3$.

I—I want to solve for N, so I need to find out what is in 1 group, the coefficient, of N.

S—I have to simplify N first, so I add 1N and 2N. I end up with 3 groups of N. On the same side as the N, I have a +9. That means that first I will have to subtract 9 from both sides and then divide each side of the equation by 3 groups.

O—I draw a −9, a divisor line, and 3 groups on both sides.

L—Let's calculate.

A—Answer the unknown side: I have +9 − 9 tallies. They are opposite signs, so I cross out an equal number of tallies from both numbers. I am left with no tallies: zero. Next, I divide the coefficient 3 groups by 3 groups. 1 divided by 1 is 1. I am left with +1N.

T—Total the other side: 3 tallies −9 tallies. They are opposite, so I cross out an equal number of tallies from each group. I am left with −6 tallies.

Next, I divide the 6 tallies by 3 groups. The answer is 2 tallies per group. The negative sign remains.

E—The answer is $1N = -2$.

17b) Let's set up the problem as it is written: $15 = -4 + 3H - H$.

I—I want to solve for H, so I need to find out what is in 1 group of H.

S—I need to simplify for H first, so I calculate 3 groups of H minus 1 group of H. I am left with 2 groups of H. In addition, -4 is on the same side of H, and I want to get rid of that. To do so, I add 4 tallies to each side. Next, I will divide each side of the equation by the coefficient, 2 groups.

O—First I add 4 tallies to both sides, and then I draw a divisor line and 2 groups on both sides.

L—Let's calculate.

A—Answer the unknown side: -4 tallies $+4$ tallies work in opposite directions on a number line. So I will cross out an equal number from each group. The answer is zero. Next, I divide 2 groups by 2 groups and the answer is 1. I circle both groups to show this.

T—Total the other side: 15 tallies plus 4 tallies equals 19 tallies.

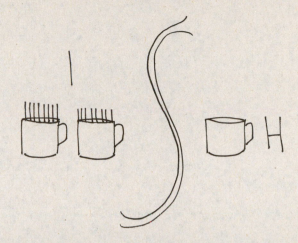

Then I divide the 19 tallies into 2 groups. In this case, I draw 9 tallies in each group with 1 tally left over.

E—The answer is 9 tallies per group and 1 tally that needs to go into 2 groups: 9½ tallies per group. 1H = 9½.

17c) Let's set up the problem as it is written: 10 + 6 = 2Y − 3Y.

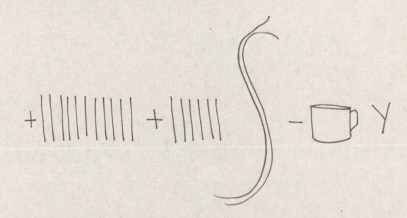

I—I want to solve for Y, so I need to find out what is in 1 group of Y.

S—I first need to simplify for Y: 2 groups of Y − 3 groups of Y is −1 group of Y. I need to divide both sides of the equation by −1 group of Y.

O—I draw a divisor line, 1 group, and a negative sign on both sides.

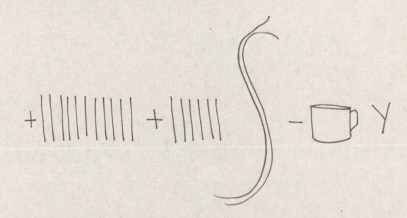

L—Let's calculate.

A—Answer the unknown side: 1 group divided by 1 group is 1. A negative divided by a negative is a positive. Thus, I have 1Y.

T—Total the other side: 10 tallies +6 tallies is 16 tallies. Next, I divide those 16 tallies by −1 group. First, 16 tallies go into one group. Second, the negative sign remains.

E—The answer is Y = −16.

17d) Let's set up the problem as it is written: 12 = T5 − T + 4.

I—I want to solve for T, so I need to find out what is in 1 group of T.

S—First, I must simplify the T's. I have 5 groups of T minus 1 group of T. I am left with 4 groups of T. Next, I have +4 on the same side of the unknown. I will have to subtract 4 from both sides and then divide each side by +4 groups.

O—I place + 4 tallies, a divisor line, and 4 groups on both sides.

L—Let's calculate.

A—Answer the unknown side: +4 − 4 equals 0. Next, 4 groups divided by 4 groups is 1 group. I have 1 group of T.

T—Total the other side: 12 tallies minus 4 tallies is 8 tallies.
Next, I divide those 8 tallies by 4 groups. I am left with 2 tallies per group.

E—I am left with 2 = 1T.

Guided Practice

In this section, I will go through the steps for the first two and you will complete them with me step-by-step. By the last two, you will work at least one step ahead of me.

Go through each step by asking what to do and doing it as close to simultaneously with the students as possible.

17e) $-4 = 8 - C(3)$

I—I want to solve for what variable? But there is a new way the coefficient is represented. Why is it okay that the coefficient is in parentheses? Yes, because the coefficient is multiplied by the variable. This means it is 3C. The subtraction symbol beforehand makes it a $-3C$.

S—Since there is only one set of C on the right side, I do not have to simplify the variable sets first. Now I must remove the 8. To do that, I subtract 8 from both sides of the equation. *Draw -8 tallies on both sides.* Next, I work with the coefficient, -3. I will divide each side by -3 groups. *Draw the steps accordingly.*

O—What did I place on both sides? *Are the two sides balanced?*

L—Let's calculate.

A—Answer the unknown side: $8 - 8$ equals 0, so I cross those 2 sets out. -3 divided by -3 is 1. Thus, I have 1C.

T—Total the other side: -4 tallies $- 8$ tallies is -12 tallies altogether. Next, I divide the -12 tallies into 3 groups also with a negative sign.

E—The answer is what? Yes, $1C = +4$ tallies, or 4. What happened to the negative symbols? That is correct, a negative divided by another negative is not a negative but a positive.

17f) $-2W + W - 2 = 7$

I—I want to solve for what variable?

S—Since there are 2 sets of W on the left side, I will simplify that first. $-2W + W$ is -1 cup of W. Now that we know the coefficient, I can more easily solve for W. To isolate the W, I must move the -2. To do so I add 2 from both sides. *Draw 2 tallies on both sides.* Next, I work with the coefficient, -1. I will divide each side by a -1 group. *Draw the groups, signs, and divisors on both sides of the equation.*

O—What do I place on both sides? Are they balanced?

L—Let's calculate.

A—Answer the unknown side: $-2 + 2$ equals 0, so I cross those pieces out. -1 divided by -1 is 1. Thus, I have 1W.

T—Total the other side: $7 + 2$ is 9. Next, I divide the 9 into 1 cup with a negative. *Move sticks accordingly.*

E—The answer is what? Yes, $1W = -9$ tallies per cup, or -9.

Now it is your turn to work one step ahead of me.

For g) and h), go through ISOLATE one step at a time, having students perform the step first. Then, check their work and go accordingly.

17g) $2G + G + G2 = 2 + 3$

17h) $2W + W = 13 + 3$

Independent Practice

Now it is your turn. Complete these four problems on your own concretely. I will be walking around to assess how you are doing but not necessarily to help.

i) $P4 - 2P = -12 + 8$ j) $5X - X = 11 + 6 - 1$

k) $12 + 2 = 4P + 3P$ l) $12 = 7Y - Y5 + 6$

Problem Solving

Let's try a couple of these together.
    Read the problem.

m) Chuck brings home 2 paychecks from last week. He adds these to the previous 5 paychecks. He now has made $14 (in thousands). How much is each paycheck?

1. Set up the equation and solve.
2. Answer the equation. Go through the steps to ISOLATE pictorially. Does the answer make sense, and why?

    Read the problem.

n) Marsha cleaned 3 garages on Saturday and 2 garages on Monday. She made $15 on Saturday and $5 on Monday. What is the average amount she earned for each garage cleaned?

1. Set up and solve the equation.
2. Answer the equation. Go through the steps to ISOLATE pictorially. Does the answer make sense, and why?

Student **LESSON # 18**

Abstract

Describe/Model

a) $\dfrac{72}{8} = -4Y + Y3$

b) $12 - 6 = \dfrac{12}{M}$

Guided Practice

c) $36 + 12 = 12 - 2W - W$

d) $-3(5) = -2C - C3$

Independent Practice

e) $3W = \dfrac{54}{9} + 3$

f) $-X - 2X = -17 + 2$

g) $6W - 4(W) = \dfrac{36}{6} + 8$

h) $75 - 3 = 12Y - Y - Y - Y$

i) $9 = -Y - 8Y$

j) $12N - 5N - 5 = 13 + 10$

k) $\dfrac{4}{V} = 1 + 3$

l) $7K - 2K = 11(2) + 3$

Problem Solving

m) Your sister gave you money for your birthday. Your mom gave you 2 times as much as your sister. Together they gave you $15 total. How much did each person give you? Set up the equation and solve.

n) Mario sold 5 boxes of books to one man and 2 boxes of books to another. He sold a total of 5 times 7 books altogether. How many books total did he sell? Set up the equation and solve.

Teaching **LESSON # 18**
Abstract

Purpose: Now that you have shown you can work through the procedures concretely and pictorially, today we will work through similar problems using only numbers and symbols. Through practice you should gain speed and accuracy with solving more complex equations. Like before, we will be simplifying the variable expression and then solving for that variable. Be careful here, as there are some more difficult calculations and steps from previous lessons here.

Let's get started.

Describe/Model

18a) $72/8 = -4Y + Y3$

I—I want to solve for Y, so I need to find out what is in 1 group, the coefficient, of Y.

S—I have to simplify Y first, so I add $-4Y$ and $Y3$, or $3Y$. I end up with $-1Y$. Now I must divide both sides by -1.

O—Are the sides balanced?

L—Let's calculate

A—Answer the unknown side: I have -1 divided by -1, which is 1. I am left with $+1Y$.

T—Total the other side: First, 72 divided by 8 is 9. Next I divided 9 by -1. That answer is -9.

E—The answer is $1Y = -9$.

18b) $12 - 6 = 12/M$

I—I want to solve for M, so I need to find out what is in 1 M. However, the M is in the denominator, so we will have to move it first.

S—Since 1M is in the denominator and I want it in the numerator, I will multiply both sides by 1M.

O—Are both sides organized to balance?

L—Let's calculate.

A—Answer the unknown side. Let's go from the original side of M: 12M divided by M is 12.

T—First on this side was $12 - 6$. That equals 6. Next I am to multiply it by M. That leaves me with 6M.

We now have $6M = 12$.

We are not done yet so I will go back to S.

S—I want to know what is in 1 M, so I divide each side by the coefficient, 6.

O—I draw a divisor and 6 on both sides.

L—I calculate.

A—6M divided by 6 is 1M.

T—Total the other side: 12 divided by 6 is 2.

E—The answer is $1M = 2$.

Guided Practice

In this section, I will go through the steps for the first problem with you and you will lead me through the second problem.

Go through each step by asking what to do and doing it as close to simultaneously with them as possible.

18c) $36 + 12 = 12 - 2W - W$

> I—I want to solve for what variable?
>
> S—What should I do first? Yes. Since there are two sets of W on the right side, I have to simplify the variable. $-2W - 1W$ means I have $-3W$. *Rewrite equation.*
>
> Now that the variable and coefficient are simplified, I must solve for 1W. What must I do now? Yes, I must subtract 12 from both sides of the equation. *Write -12 on both sides.*
>
> Then what must happen to both sides? Yes, I must divide by the coefficient, -3. I will divide each side by -3 groups. Write *the steps accordingly.*
>
> O—What did I place on both sides? Are the two sides balanced?
>
> L—Let's calculate.
>
> A—Answer the unknown side. $12 - 12$ equals 0. -3 divided by -3 is 1. Thus, I have 1W.
>
> T—Total the other side: $36 - 12$ is 24. Next, I divide the 24 by -3.
>
> E—The answer is what? Yes, $1W = -8$.

Now it is your turn to work one step ahead of me.

For d), go through ISOLATE one step at a time having students perform the step first. Then, check their work and adjust instruction or move to independent practice accordingly.

18d) $-3(5) = -2C - C3$

Independent Practice

Now it is your turn. Complete these eight problems on your own without help. I will be walking around to assess how you are doing but not necessarily to help.

e) $3W = \dfrac{54}{9} + 3$ f) $-X - 2X = -17 + 2$

g) $6W - 4(W) = \dfrac{36}{6} + 8$ h) $75 - 3 = 12Y - Y - Y - Y$

i) $9 = -Y - 8Y$ j) $12N - 5N - 5 = 13 + 10$

k) $\dfrac{4}{V} = 1 + 3$ l) $7K - 2K = 11(2) + 3$

Problem Solving

Let's try a couple of these together.
  Read the problem.

m) Your sister gave you money for your birthday. Your mom gave you 2 times as much as your sister. Together they gave you $15 total. How much did each person give you?

1. Set up the equation and solve.
2. Answer the equation. Go through the steps to ISOLATE. Does the answer make sense, and why?

Read the problem.

n) Mario sold 5 boxes of books to one man and 2 boxes of books to another. He sold a total of 5 times 7 books altogether. How many books total did he sell?

1. Set up the equation and solve.
2. Answer the equation. Go through the steps to ISOLATE. Does the answer make sense, and why?

Student **LESSON # 19**

Abstract II

Describe/Model

a) $8P - 2P = 32$

b) $\dfrac{15}{C} = \dfrac{10}{2}$

Guided Practice

c) $\dfrac{42}{7W} = 2$

d) $2(8) = 3M + 9M$

Independent Practice

e) $7(W) - 3W = \dfrac{18}{2}$

f) $44 = 8P - 2P + 20$

g) $2N + 6(N) = 35$

h) $\dfrac{60}{5} = 5Y + Y$

i) $\dfrac{10}{K} = \dfrac{35}{7}$

j) $10F - F + 1F - 4 = 36$

k) $\dfrac{36}{6} = \dfrac{24}{V}$

l) $\dfrac{14X}{2} - 6X = 30 + 10$

Problem Solving

m) Eric paid $40 for the movies with his friends. He paid the extra cost for the popcorn and the drinks. The total cost was $56. How much did Eric spend on popcorn and drinks? Set up and solve the equation.

n) List the steps to solving for an unknown quantity.

Teaching **LESSON # 19**
Abstract II

Purpose: Today we will work more on solving for unknowns by first simplifying expressions. Be careful, as there are fractions in some of the answers. As you know, seldom outside of a math textbook do answers come in whole numbers.

Let's get started.

Describe/Model

19a) $8P - 2P = 32$

I—I want to solve for P, so I need to find out what is in 1 group, the coefficient, of P.

S—I have to simplify P first, so I compute $8P - 2P$ to find 6P. Now I must divide both sides by 6.

O—Are the sides balanced?

L—Let's calculate.

A—Answer the unknown side. I have 6 divided by 6, which is 1. I am left with +1P.

T—Total the other side: 32 divided by 6 is 5 with 2 remaining. That means $6\frac{2}{6}$, which can be simplified to $6\frac{1}{3}$.

E—The answer is $1P = 6\frac{1}{3}$.

19b) $\dfrac{15}{C} = \dfrac{10}{2}$

I—I want to solve for C, so I need to find out what is in 1C. However, the C is in the denominator, so we will have to move it first.

S—Since 1C is in the denominator and I want it in the numerator, I will multiply both sides by 1C.

O—Are both sides organized to balance?

L—Let's calculate.

A—Answer the unknown side. Let's go from the original side of C: 15C/C is 15.

T—On the other side was 10/2. That equals 5. Next I am to multiply it by C. That leaves me with 5C.

We now have $15 = 5C$.

We are not done yet, so I will go back to S.

S—I want to know what is in 1 C so I divide each side by the coefficient, 5.

O—I divide both sides by 5.

L—Let's calculate.

A—5C divided by 5 is 1C.

T—Total the other side: 15 divided by 5 is 3.

E—The answer is $1C = 3$.

Guided Practice

In this section, I will go through the steps for the first problem with you and you will lead me through the second problem.

Go through each step by asking what to do and doing it as close to simultaneously with the students as possible.

19c) $\dfrac{42}{7W} = 2$

I—What do I want to solve for? Yes, I want to solve for W, so I need to find out what is in 1 W. However, the W is in the denominator, so we will have to move it first.

S—Since 7W is in the denominator, what should I do? Yes, I want it in the numerator, so I will multiply both sides by 7W.

O—Are both sides organized to balance?

L—Let's calculate.

A—Answer the unknown side. *Wait for students to solve this.* Let's go from the original side of W: 7W(42) divided by 7W is 42.

T—On the other side is 2 times 7W. *Wait for students to work through problem.* That equals 14W.

We now have 42 = 7W.

We are not done yet, so I will go back to S.

S—I want to know what is in 1 W, so what do I do? Yes, I divide each side by the coefficient, 7.

O—I divide both sides by 7.

L—Let's calculate.

A—*Initiate student work.* 7W divided by 7 is 1W.

T—Total the other side. *Initiate student work.* 42 divided by 7 is 6.

E—The answer is 1W = 6.

Now it is your turn to work one step ahead of me.

For d), go through ISOLATE one step at a time, having students perform the step first. Then, check their work and adjust instruction or move to independent practice accordingly.

d) $2(8) = 3M + 9M$

Independent Practice

Now it is your turn. Complete these eight problems on your own without help. I will be walking around to assess how you are doing but not necessarily to help.

e) $7(W) - 3W = \dfrac{18}{2}$ f) $44 = 8P - 2P + 20$

g) $2N + 6(N) = 35$ h) $\dfrac{60}{5} = 5Y + Y$

i) $\dfrac{10}{K} = \dfrac{35}{7}$ j) $10F - F + 1F - 4 = 36$

k) $\dfrac{36}{6} = \dfrac{24}{V}$ l) $\dfrac{14X}{2} - 6X = 30 + 10$

Problem Solving

Try this word problem.
 Read the problem

m) Eric paid $40 for the movies with his friends. He paid the extra cost for the popcorn and the drinks. The total cost was $56. How much did Eric spend on popcorn and drinks?

1. Set up and solve the equation.
    What should you do first?

2. Does the answer make sense, and why?

n) List the steps to solving for an unknown quantity.

Look for students to go through the steps of ISOLATE with some possible variations due to several constraints as seen in the problems above.

Student   **LESSON # 20**

Fluency/Work Fast

$6(R) - 3R = \dfrac{24}{2}$ $15 = 8R - 2R - 3$

$5R + 2(R) = 35$ $\dfrac{30}{5} = 2R + 4R$

$\dfrac{35}{7} + 3 = 4X$ $-2X - X = -17 + -10$

$2X - 3(X) = 20 - 8$ $80 + 1 = 12X - X - X - X$

$\dfrac{24}{6} = \dfrac{8}{N}$ $\dfrac{2N}{3} = 10 + 2$

$-9 = -4V - 5V$ $11 + 10 = 10V - 7V$

$\dfrac{12}{V} = 3 + 3$ $4V - 2V = 25 - 5$

$5Y + 5(Y) = 50$ $\dfrac{30}{6} = 5Y$

$\dfrac{8}{Y} = \dfrac{40}{5}$ $3Y - 6Y = -24$

Teaching **LESSON # 20**

Fluency/Work Fast

Note: This is a mixed review of solving equations. Some problems include simplifying expressions and others do not.

Now that you have shown that you know how to solve multistep equations, let's see how many accurate answers you can give in a 2-minute timed quiz. The problems in this quiz are all different, so read each problem carefully. We will start with this one. *(Point to any problem on the sheet.)* Once you give an answer, do not stop; go to the next question on the sheet to the right, or return to the next line below. Answer every question. If you skip a question, that counts as incorrect. If you happen to come to the last problem on the sheet, continue with the problem at the top of the paper and do not stop. *(Run finger across and down the lines of problems to read like a paragraph.)* I will stop you 2 minutes after I say go.

Ready? Go:

Student   **LESSON # 21**

Concrete/Hands-on: Solving for a Variable When Like Variables Are on Opposite Sides

Describe/Model

a) $X = 3X + 4$

b) $3X - 8 = X$

c) $1N = 4N - 9$

d) $3Y = 10 - 2Y$

Guided Practice

e) $Y = 2Y - 3$

f) $6 + N = -N$

g) $3X = 12 - X$

h) $N = -N + 8$

Independent Practice

i) $14 - Y = Y$

j) $X + 7 = 2X$

k) $2Y + 9 = 3Y$

l) $X = 6 - 2X$

Problem Solving

m) Tom had $20 (20) added (+) to his usual pay (X). He now has (=) 2 times what he is normally paid (2X). What is his normal pay? Set up the equation and solve.

n) Carrie had $12 (12). Some money was taken away (−Y). She ended up (=) with the same amount that was taken away from her (Y). Set up the equation and solve.

Teaching **LESSON # 21**

Concrete/Hands-on: Solving for a Variable When Like Variables Are on Opposite Sides

Purpose: When we solved for variables and unknowns in the last set of lessons, we first had to simplify the variable sets in the equation. In this set of lessons, we will do the same thing but across the equal sign. This will require some good organization. The steps to ISOLATE work here as well, but we have an extra thought in the S step. To isolate the variable or unknown, we will need to move a variable.

Relevance: When unknowns are presented in questions and potential answers, we must be smart in how we tackle the problem. On a smaller scale, if I found money and turned it in as a lost item, I might receive a fraction of that money as a reward. At work, if I sold shoes, I would first have to determine how many shoes to buy before I knew how much I could charge for them.

Again, there are unknowns in not only the question but also in the answer I am trying to achieve. The purpose of this set of lessons is to help us understand how to work with such equations, which will prepare us for our future.

Let's get started.

Describe/Model

21a) Let's set up the problem as it is written: X = 3X + 4.

I—I want to solve for X, so I need to find out what is in 1 cup, the coefficient, of X.

S—I have more than 1 set of X across the equal sign, so I will have to simplify the variables. In this case, 3X is with another number, so it would be best to move the 3X to help isolate it. Thus, I subtract 3X from both sides.

O—I place a minus sign, 3 cups, and an X on both sides

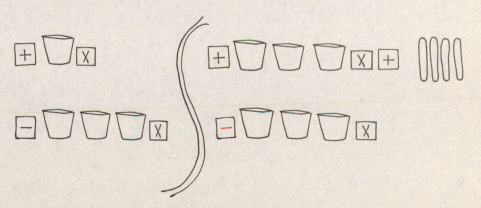

L—Let's calculate.

A—Answer the leftmost unknown side: $+1X - 3X$ is $-2X$.

T—Total the other side: $3X + 4 - 3X$ is 4.

We now have $-2X = 4$. So let's go back to S and set up the equations.

S—Divide both sides of the equation by -2.

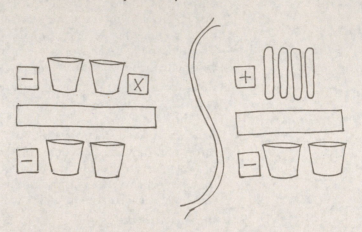

O—Organize the equations to balance.

L—Let's calculate.

A—$-2X$ divided by -2 is $1X$.

T—4 sticks divided into 2 cups with a negative sign remaining is -2 sticks per cup.

E—The answer is $1X = -2$ sticks per cup, or -2.

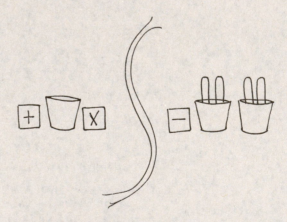

21b) Let's set up the problem as it is written: $3X - 8 = X$.

I—I want to solve for X, so I need to find out what is in 1 cup, the coefficient, of X.

S—I have more than 1 set of X across the equal sign, so I will have to simplify the variables. In this case, 3X is with another number, so it would be best to move the 3X to help isolate it. Thus, I subtract 3X from both sides.

O—I place a minus sign, 3 cups, and an X on both sides.

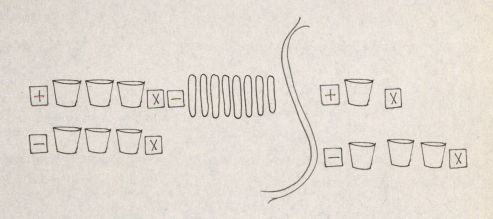

L—Let's calculate.

A—Answer the leftmost unknown side: $3X - 8 - 3X$ is -8.

T—Total the other side: $1X - 3X$ is $-2X$.

We now have $-8 = -2X$. So let's go back to S and set up the equations.

S—Divide both sides of the equation by -2.

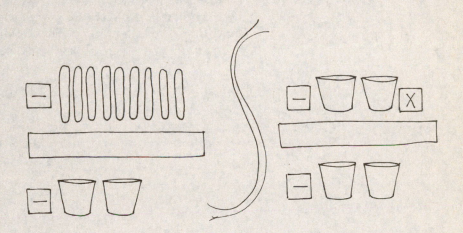

O—Organize the equations to balance.

L—Let's calculate.

A—$-2X$ divided by -2 is $1X$.

T—-8 sticks divided into 2 cups with a negative sign remaining is $+2$ sticks per cup. What happened to the two negatives? That is right, they became a positive.

E—The answer is $1X = 2$ sticks per cup, or 2.

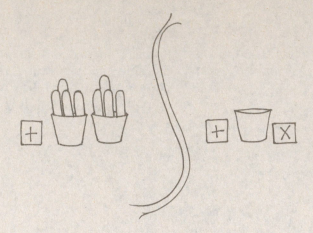

21c) Let's set up the problem as it is written: 1N = 4N − 9.

I—I want to solve for N, so I need to find out what is in 1 cup, the coefficient, of N.

S—I have more than 1 set of N across the equal sign, so I will have to simplify the variables. In this case, 4N is with another number, so it would be best to move the 4N to help isolate it. Thus, I subtract 4N from both sides.

O—I place a minus sign, 4 cups, and an N on both sides.

L—Let's calculate.

A—Answer the leftmost unknown side: 1N − 4N is −3N.

T—Total the other side: 4N − 9 − 4N is −9.

We now have −3N = −9. So let's go back to S and set up the equations.

S—Divide both sides of the equation by −3.

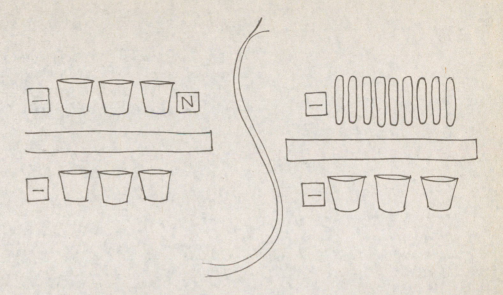

O—Organize the equations to balance.

L—Let's calculate.

A—−3N divided by −3 is 1N.

T—−9 sticks divided into 3 cups with a negative sign remaining is +3 sticks per cup. What happened to the two negatives? That is right, they became a positive.

E—The answer is 1N = 3 sticks per cup, or 3.

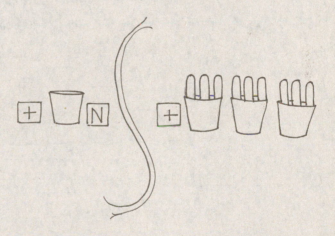

21d) Let's set up the problem as it is written: 3Y = 10 − 2Y.

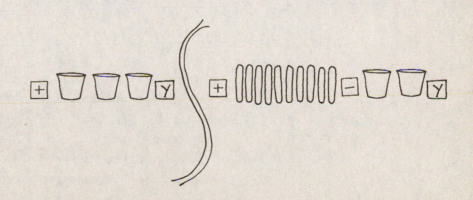

I—I want to solve for Y, so I need to find out what is in 1 cup, the coefficient, of Y.

S—I have more than 1 set of Y across the equal sign, so I will have to simplify the variables. In this case, −2Y is with another number, so it would be best to move the −2Y to help isolate it. Thus, I add 2Y to both sides.

O—I place an addition sign, 2 cups, and a Y on both sides.

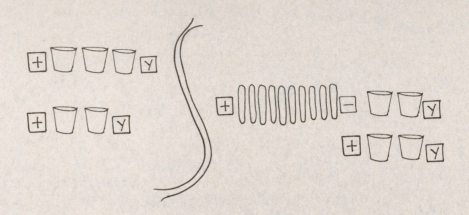

L—Let's calculate.

A—Answer the leftmost unknown side: 3Y + 2Y is 5Y.

T—Total the other side; 10 − 2Y + 2Y is 10.

We now have 5Y = 10. So let's go back to S and set up the equations.

S—Divide both sides of the equation by 5.

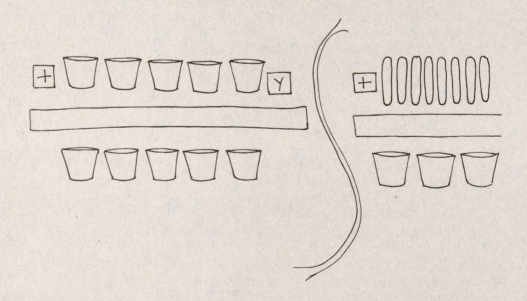

O—Organize the equations to balance.

L—Let's calculate.

A—5Y divided by 5 is 1Y.

T—10 sticks divided into 5 cups is 2 sticks per cup.

E—The answer is 1Y = 5 sticks per cup, or 5.

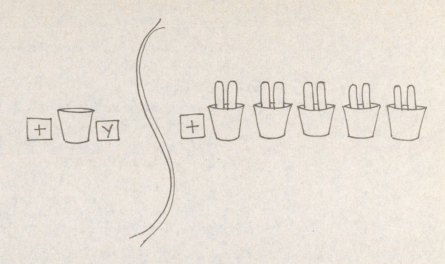

Guided Practice

In this section, I will go through the steps for the first two and you will complete them with me step-by-step. By the last two, you will work at least one step ahead of me.

Go through each step by asking what to do and doing it as close to simultaneously with them as possible.

21e) $Y = 2Y - 3$

Let's set up the problem as it is written.

I—What are we solving for? Yes, the Y.

S—I have more than 1 set of Y across the equal sign, so what should we move? Yes, the 2Y. *See that students set up subtraction of 2Y.*

O—Is the equation balanced?

L—Let's calculate.

A—Answer the leftmost unknown side. *Observe student work.*

T—Total the other side. *Observe student work.*

We now have $-1Y = -3$. So let's go back to S and set up the equations.

S—What should we do? Yes, divide both sides of the equation by −1.

O—Is the equation balanced?

L—Let's calculate.

A—Answer the unknown side. *See that students find that −1Y divided by −1 is 1Y.*

T—Total the other side. *See that students find that −3 divided by −1 is 3.*

E—The answer is what? Yes, $1Y = +3$.

21f) $6 + N = -N$

Let's set up the problem as it is written.

I—What are we solving for? Yes, the N.

S—I have more than 1 set of N across the equal sign, so what should we move? Yes, the +N. *See that students set up subtraction of 1N.*

O—Is the equation balanced?

L—Let's calculate.

A—Answer the leftmost unknown side. *Observe student work.*

T—Total the other side. *Observe student work.*

We now have $6 = -2N$. So let's go back to S and set up the equations.

S—What should we do? Yes, divide both sides of the equation by -2.

O—Is the equation balanced?

L—Let's calculate.

A—Answer the unknown side. *See that students find that $-2N$ divided by -2 is 1N.*

T—Total the other side. *See that students find that 6 divided by -2 is -3.*

E—The answer is what? Yes, $1N = -3$.

Now it is your turn to work one step ahead of me.

For g) and h), go through ISOLATE one step at a time, having students perform the step first. Then, check their work and go accordingly.

g) $3X = 12 - X$ h) $N = -N + 8$

Independent Practice

Now it is your turn. Complete these four problems on your own concretely. I will be walking around to assess how you are doing but not necessarily to help.

i) $14 - Y = Y$ j) $X + 7 = 2X$

k) $2Y + 9 = 3Y$ l) $X = 6 - 2X$

Problem Solving

Let's try a couple of these together.
  Read the problem.

m) Tom had $20 (20) added (+) to his usual pay (X). He now has (=) 2 times what he is normally paid (2X). What is his normal pay?

  1. Set up the equation and solve.
  2. Answer the equation. Go through the steps to ISOLATE concretely. Does the answer make sense, and why?

  Read the problem.

n) Carrie had $12 (12). Some money was taken away ($-Y$). She ended up (=) with the same amount that was taken away from her (Y). Set up the equation and solve.

  1. Set up and solve the equation.
  2. Answer the equation. Go through the steps to ISOLATE concretely. Does the answer make sense, and why?

Student   **LESSON # 22**

Representational/Pictures

Describe/Model

a) $T - 8 = 3T$ b) $6 - Y = Y - 8$

c) $3 - 3X = X - 9$ d) $5C - C = C + 18$

Guided Practice

e) $2 + H = -13 + 4H$ f) $7W = 3 + 4W$

g) $-3 + F = 2F + 8$ h) $16 + V = 3V + 2$

Independent Practice

i) $-P - 7 = 5 + 5P$ j) $12 - 2T = -3 + T$

k) $5 + Y = 3Y - 3$ l) $8 + 2X = 5X + 2$

Problem Solving

m) The price of 1 CD (N) plus $15 (+15) is (=) the same as 2 CDs (2N) plus $3. How much does 1 CD cost? Set up the equation and solve.

Teaching **LESSON # 22**
Representational/Pictures

Purpose: Yesterday we worked on solving for unknowns across an equal sign using hands-on materials. Today we will complete the same procedures but using pictures of the steps instead of using the materials.

Let's get started.

Describe/Model

22a) Let's set up the problem as it is written: T − 8 = 3T.

I—I want to solve for T, so I need to find out what is in 1 group, the coefficient, of T.

S—I have more than 1 set of T across the equal sign, so I will have to simplify the variables. In this case, 1T is with another number, so it would be best to move the 1T to help isolate it. Thus, I subtract 1T from both sides.

O—I draw a minus sign and 1 group of T on both sides.

L—Let's calculate.
A—Answer the leftmost unknown side: 1T − 8 − 1T is −8.
T—Total the other side: 3T − 1T is 2T.

We now have −8 = 2T. So let's go back to S and set up the equations.

S—Divide both sides of the equation by 2.

O—Organize the equations to balance.

L—Let's calculate.

A—2T divided by 2 is 1T.

T—−8 tallies divided into 2 groups is −4 tallies per group.

E—The answer is 1T = −4, or −4.

22b) Let's set up the problem as it is written: 6 − Y = Y − 8.

I—I want to solve for Y, so I need to find out what is in 1 group, the coefficient, of Y.

S—I have more than 1 set of Y across the equal sign, so I will have to simplify the variables. In this case, I will subtract 1Y from the right side of the equation.

O—I draw a minus sign and 1 group of Y on both sides.

L—Let's calculate.

A—Answer the leftmost unknown side: $6 - 1Y - 1Y$ is $6 - 2Y$.

T—Total the other side: $1Y - 8 - 1Y$ is -8.

We now have $6 - 2Y = -8$. So let's go back to S and set up the equations.

S—To isolate the Y, I need to first subtract 6 from both sides of the equation.

That leaves me with $-2Y = -14$.

Then I need to divide both sides of the equation by Y's coefficient, -2.

O—Organize the equations to balance.

L—Let's calculate.

A—−2Y divided by −2 is 1Y.

T—−14 tallies divided into −2 groups is +7 tallies per group. Remember the rule for negatives.

E—The answer is 1Y = 7.

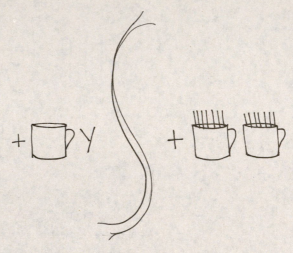

22c) Let's set up the problem as it is written: 3 − 3X = X − 9.

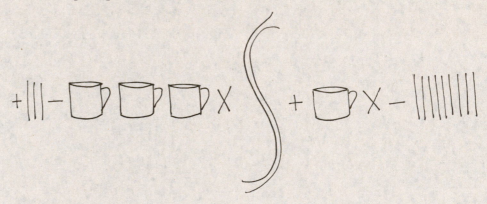

I—I want to solve for X, so I need to find out what is in one group, the coefficient, of X.

S—I have more than one set of X across the equal sign so I will have to simplify the variables. In this case, I will subtract 1X from the right side of the equation.

O—I draw a minus sign and 1 group of X on both sides.

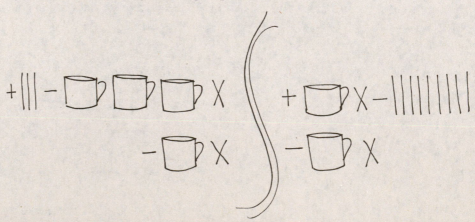

L—Let's calculate.

A—Answer the leftmost unknown side: 3 − 3X − 1X is 3 − 4X.

T—Total the other side: 1X − 9 − 1X is −9.

We now have 3 − 4X = −9. So let's go back to S and set up the equations.

S—To isolate the X, I need to first subtract 3 from both sides of the equation.

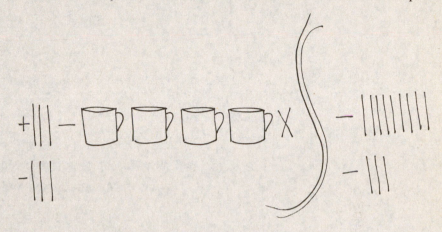

That leaves me −4X = −12.

Next, I need to divide both sides of the equation by X's coefficient −4.

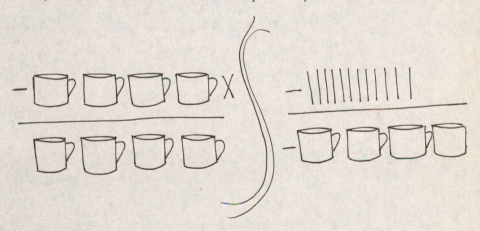

O—Organize the equations to balance.

L—Let's calculate.

A—−4X divided by −4 is 1X.

T—−12 tallies divided into −4 groups is +3 tallies per group. Remember the rule for negatives.

E—The answer is 1X = 3.

22d) Let's set up the problem as it is written: 5C − 1C = 1C + 18.

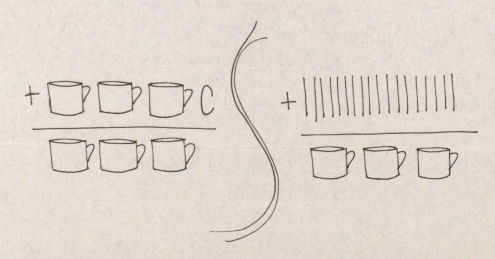

I—I want to solve for C, so I need to find out what is in 1 group, the coefficient, of C.

S—I have more than 1 set of C on the left side of the equal sign. 5 groups of C minus 1 group of C is 4 groups of C. Now I have 4C = 1C + 18. Still, I have sets of C across the equal sign, so I will have to simplify the variables. In this case, I will subtract 1C from the right side of the equation.

O—I draw a minus sign and 1 group of C on both sides.

L—Let's calculate.

A—Answer the leftmost unknown side: 4C − 1C is 3C.

T—Total the other side: 1C + 18 − 1C is 18.

We now have 3C = 18. So let's go back to S and set up the equations.

S—To isolate the C, I need to divide both sides of the equation by C's coefficient, 3.

O—Organize the equations to balance.

L—Let's calculate.

A—3C divided by 3 is 1C.

T—18 tallies divided into 3 groups is 6 tallies per group.

E—The answer is 1C = 6.

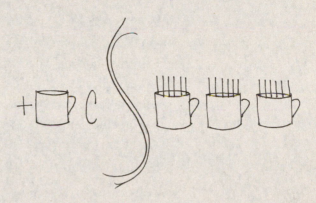

Guided Practice

In this section, I will go through the steps for the first two and you will complete them with me step-by-step. By the last two, you will work at least one step ahead of me.

Go through each step by asking what to do and doing it as close to simultaneously with the students as possible.

22e) 2 + 1H = −13 + 4H

Let's set up the problem as it is written.

I—What are we solving for? Yes, the H.

S—I have more than 1 set of H across the equal sign, so what should we move? Yes, the 4H. *See that students set up subtraction of 4H.*

O—Is the equation balanced?

L—Let's calculate.

A—Answer the leftmost unknown side. *Observe student work.*

T—Total the other side. *Observe student work.*

We now have 2 + −3H = −13. So let's go back to S and set up the equations.

S—What should we do? Yes, first we subtract 2 from both sides of the equation. Then we divide both sides by −3. *See that students set up the equations.*

O—Is the equation balanced?

L—Let's calculate.

A—Answer the unknown side. *See that students subtract 2, divide by −3, and are left with 1H.*

T—Total the other side. *See that students subtract 2 from −13 to get −15 then divide −15 by −3 to get +5.*

E—The answer is what? Yes, 1H = +5.

22f) 7W = 3 + 4W.

Let's set up the problem as it is written.

I—What are we solving for? Yes, the W.

S—I have more than 1 set of W across the equal sign, so what should we move? Yes, the + 4W. *See that students set up subtraction of 4W.*

O—Is the equation balanced?

L—Let's calculate.

A—Answer the leftmost unknown side. *Observe student work.*

T—Total the other side. *Observe student work.*

We now have 3W = 3. So let's go back to S and set up the equations.

S—What should we do? Yes, divide both sides of the equation by 3.

O—Is the equation balanced?

L—Let's calculate.

A—Answer the unknown side. *See that students find that 3W divided by 3 is 1W.*

T—Total the other side. *See that students find that 3 divided by 3 is 1.*

E—The answer is what? Yes, 1W = 1.

Now it is your turn to work one step ahead of me.

For g) and h), go through ISOLATE one step at a time, having students perform the step first. Then, check their work and go accordingly.

g) $-3 + F = 2F + 8$ h) $16 + V = 3V + 2$

Independent Practice

Now it is your turn. Complete these four problems on your own concretely. I will be walking around to assess how you are doing but not necessarily to help.

i) $-P - 7 = 5 + 5P$ j) $12 - 2T = -3 + T$

k) $5 + Y = 3Y - 3$ l) $8 + 2X = 5X + 2$

Problem Solving

Let's try a couple of these together.
    Read the problem.

m) The price of 1 CD (N) plus \$15 (+15) is (=) the same as 2 CDs (2N) plus \$3. How much does 1 CD cost?

1. Set up the equation and solve.
2. Answer the equation. Go through the steps to ISOLATE pictorially. Does the answer make sense, and why?

Student **LESSON # 23**

Abstract

Describe/Model

    a) $8 + 4Y = Y - 22$ b) $2K + 3K = 11 + 2 + 4K$

Guided Practice

    c) $5 - 4W = -9 + 3W$ d) $-7X - 13 = 7X + 1$

Independent Practice

    e) $P - 18 = 2P + 2$ f) $-14 + 6M = 11 + M$

    g) $8F - 16 = 2F + 26$ h) $11 - 5C = -22 + 6C$

    i) $15 - 2D = -12 + 7D$ j) $8U + U - 17 = U + 7$

    k) $27 + 2Y = 7Y + 2$ l) $19W + 16 = 7W - 8$

Problem Solving

    m) Two brothers were given an equal amount of money and bought equally priced video games. Brandon bought 1 game for himself and had $12 left. Taylor bought 2 games and had $0 left. Since both brothers had the same amount of money, how much did each video game cost? Set up the equation and solve.

Teaching LESSON # 23

Abstract

Purpose: Yesterday we worked on solving for unknowns across an equal sign using pictorial representations. Today we will complete the same procedures but using number and symbols. This will help us apply more speed to the accuracy we established in the previous lessons

Let's get started.

Describe/Model

23a) $8 + 4Y = Y - 22$

I—I want to solve for Y, so I need to find out what is in 1 group, the coefficient, of Y.

S—I have more than 1 set of Y across the equal sign, so I will have to simplify the variables. In this case, 1Y is with another number, so it would be best to move the 1Y to help isolate it. Thus, I subtract 1Y from both sides.

O—I organize the equations to be balanced.

L—Let's calculate.

A—Answer the leftmost unknown side: $8 + 4Y - 1Y = 8 + 3Y$.

T—Total the other side. $1Y - 22 - 1Y = -22$.

We now have $8 + 3Y = -22$. So let's go back to S and set up the equations.

S—I must subtract 8 from both sides to isolate the Y.

Then I must divide both sides of the equation by 3.

O—Organize the equations to balance.

L—Let's calculate.

A—$8 + 3Y - 8 = 3Y$; $3Y/3 = 1Y$

T—$-22 - 8 = -30$; $-30/3 = -10$

E—The answer is $Y = -10$.

23b) $2K + 3K = 11 + 2 + 4K$

I—I want to solve for K, so I need to find out what is in 1 group, the coefficient, of K.

S—I have more than 1 set of K on the left side of the equation: $2K + 3K = 5K$. Now I have $5K = 11 + 2 + 4K$. I still have sets of K across the equal sign, so I will have to simplify the variables. In this case, 4K is with another number, so it would be best to move the 4K to help isolate it. Thus, I subtract 4K from both sides.

O—I organize the equations to be balanced.

L—Let's calculate.

A—Answer the leftmost unknown side: $5K - 4K = 1K$.

T—Total the other side: $11 + 2 + 4K - 4K = 13$.

We now have $1K = 13$. So let's go back to S and set up the equations.

S—I must divide both sides of the equation by 1.

O—Organize the equations to balance.

L—Let's calculate.

A—$1K/1 = 1K$

T—$13/1 = 13$

E—The answer is $K = 13$

Guided Practice

In this section, I will go through the steps for these two problems with you. For the first one I will lead. For the second one you will lead.

Go through each step by asking what to do and doing it as close to simultaneously with the students as possible.

23c) $5 - 4W = -9 + 3W$

Let's set up the problem as it is written.

I—What are we solving for? Yes, the W.

S—I have more than 1 set of W across the equal sign, so what should we move? Yes, the 3W works. *See that students set up subtraction of 3W.*

Note: If the you and the students choose to add 4W, then the procedures that follow will not coordinate your steps.

O—Is the equation balanced?

L—Let's calculate.

A—Answer the leftmost unknown side. *Observe student work.*

T—Total the other side. *Observe student work.*

We now have $5 - 7W = -9$. So let's go back to S and set up the equations.

S—What should we do? Yes, first we subtract 5 from both sides of the equation. Then we divide both sides by -7. *See that students set up the equations.*

O—Is the equation balanced?

L—Let's calculate.

A—Answer the unknown side. *See that students subtract 5, divide by -7, and are left with 1W.*

T—Total the other side. *See that students subtract 5 from -9 to get -14 then divide -14 by -7 to get $+2$.*

E—The answer is what? Yes, $1W = +2$.

Now it is your turn to work one step ahead of me.

For d), go through ISOLATE one step at a time having students perform the step first. Then, check their work and go accordingly.

d) $-14 + 6M = 11 + 1M$

Independent Practice

Now it is your turn. Complete these four problems on your own concretely. I will be walking around to assess how you are doing but not necessarily to help.

e) $P - 18 = 2P + 2$ f) $-14 + 6M = 11 + M$

g) $8F - 16 = 2F + 26$ h) $11 - 5C = -22 + 6C$

i) $15 - 2D = -12 + 7D$ j) $8U + U - 17 = U + 7$

k) $27 + 2Y = 7Y + 2$ l) $19W + 16 = 7W - 8$

Problem Solving

m) Two brothers were given an equal amount of money and bought equally priced video games. Brandon bought one game for himself and had $12 left. Taylor bought 2 games and had $0 left. Since both brothers had the same amount of money, how much did each video game cost?

1. Set up the equation and solve.

2. Answer the equation. Go through the steps to ISOLATE. Does the answer make sense, and why?

Student **LESSON # 24**

Abstract II

Describe/Model

a) $\dfrac{T}{2} - 3 = T + 1$ b) $\dfrac{P}{2} + 2 = 2P - 8$

Guided Practice

c) $13 - X = \dfrac{6X}{3} - 8$ d) $-5 + M = \dfrac{1M}{3} + 1$

Independent Practice

e) $X + 8 = 26 - 2X$ f) $\dfrac{K}{7} + 5 = 2$

g) $21 - X = 2X - 3$ h) $30 + X = 3X$

i) $-4 + Y + 2Y = 17$ j) $-23 + 6R = 1$

k) $2N - 8 = \dfrac{1N}{2} - 2$ l) $15C - 12 = 13 + 10C$

m) $-3B - 8 = B + 8$ n) $2N + N + 12 = 3 + N + 10$

Problem Solving

o) You fill a lawnmower with an unknown number of gallons of gas. You know it goes for about 3/2 hours per gallon. If the mower runs for 6 hours until it is empty, how many gallons does it hold?

Teaching **LESSON # 24**
Abstract II

Purpose: Yesterday we worked on solving for unknowns across an equal sign using only numbers and symbols. Today we will complete the same procedures, but the work becomes a bit tougher. Be careful, as there is much more computation, including fractions, embedded in each problem.

Let's get started.

Describe/Model

24a) $1T/2 - 3 = 1T + 1$

I—I want to solve for T, so I need to find out what is in 1T.

S—I have more than 1 set of T across the equal sign, so I will have to simplify the variables. In this case, 1T is with another number, so it would be best to move the 1T to help isolate it. Thus, I subtract 1T from both sides.

O—I organize the equations to be balanced.

L—Let's calculate.

A—Answer the leftmost unknown side: $1T/2 - 3 - 1T = -1T/2 - 3$.

T—Total the other side: $1T + 1 - 1T = +1$.

We now have $-1T/2 - 3 = +1$. So let's go back to S and set up the equations.

S—I must add 3 from both sides to isolate T.

Then, I must multiply both sides by 2 and divide each side by −1.

O—Organize the equations to balance: $(-2/1)(-1T/2) - 3 + 3 = (+1 + 3)(-2/1)$

L—Let's calculate.

A—$(-2/1)(-1T/2) - 3 + 3 = 1T$

T—$(+1 + 3)(-2/1) = -8$

E—The answer is $1T = -8$

24b) $-5 + 1M = 1M/3 + 1$

I—I want to solve for M, so I need to find out what is in 1M.

S—I have more than 1 set of M across the equal sign, so I will have to simplify the variables. In this case, 1M/3 is with another number, so it would be best to move the 1M/3 to help isolate it. Thus, I subtract 1M/3 from both sides.

O—I organize the equations to be balanced.

L—Let's calculate.

A—Answer the leftmost unknown side: $-5 + 1M - 1M/3 = -5 + 2M/3$.

T—Total the other side: $1M/3 + 1 - 1M/3 = 1$.

We now have $-5 + 2M/3 = 1$. So let's go back to S and set up the equations.

S—I must add 5 to both sides to isolate the M.

Then I must multiply both sides by 3 and divide each side by 2.

O—Organize the equations to balance: $(-5 + 5) + 2M/3(3/2) = (1 + 5)(3/2)$.

L—Let's calculate.

A—(−5 + 5) + 2M/3(3/2) = 1M

T—M = (1 + 5)(3/2) = 9

E—The answer is 1M = 9.

Guided Practice

In this section, I will go through the steps for these two problems with you. For the first one I will lead. For the second one you will lead.

Go through each step by asking what to do and doing it as close to simultaneously with the students as possible.

24c) 13 − 1X = 6X/3 − 8

Let's set up the problem as it is written.

I: What are we solving for? Yes, the X.

S: First, there is a computation that I can do. What is it? Yes, 6X/3 is 2X.

Next, I have more than 1 set of X across the equal sign, so what should we move? Yes, the 2X works. *See that students set up subtraction of 2X.*

Note: *If the you and the students choose to add 1X, then the procedures that follow will not coordinate your steps.*

O—Is the equation balanced?

L—Let's calculate.

A—Answer the leftmost unknown side. *Observe student work.*

T—Total the other side. *Observe student work.*

We now have 13 − 3X = −8. So, let's go back to S and set up the equations.

S—What should we do? Yes, first we subtract 13 from both sides of the equation. Then we divide both sides by −3. *See that students set up the equations.*

O—Is the equation balanced?

L—Let's calculate.

A—Answer the unknown side. *See that students subtract 13, divide by −3, and are left with 1X.*

T—Total the other side. *See that students subtract 13 from −8 to get −21 then divide −21 by −3 to get +7.*

E—The answer is what? Yes, 1X = +7.

Now it is your turn to work one step ahead of me.

For d), go through ISOLATE one step at a time having students perform the step first. Then, check their work and go accordingly.

d) 15C − 12 = 13 + 10C

Independent Practice

Now it is your turn. Complete these four problems on your own concretely. I will be walking around to assess how you are doing but not necessarily to help. *There are many problems here, so do not expect all students to answer them in a timely fashion. Set a limit as far as expectations.*

e) X + 8 = 26 − 2X   f) $\frac{K}{7} + 5 = 2$

g) 21 − X = 2X − 3   h) 30 + X = 3X

i) $-4 + Y + 2Y = 17$ j) $-23 + 6R = 1$

k) $2N - 8 = \dfrac{1N}{2} - 2$ l) $15C - 12 = 13 + 10C$

m) $-3B - 8 = B + 8$ n) $2N + N + 12 = 3 + N + 10$

Problem Solving

o)   You fill a lawnmower with an unknown number of gallons of gas. You know it goes for about 3/2 hours per gallon. If the mower runs for 6 hours until it is empty, how many gallons does it hold?

1. Set up the equation and solve.

2. Answer the equation. Go through the steps to ISOLATE. Does the answer make sense, and why?

Student **LESSON # 25**

Fluency/Work Fast

a) $18 - Y = Y$

b) $X - 11 = 2X$

c) $2Y + 9 = 3Y$

d) $X = 6 - 2X$

e) $-P - 7 = 13 + 9P$

f) $\dfrac{P}{5} + 2 = 3P + 12$

g) $25 + Y = 5Y - 3$

h) $13 + 2X = 5X - 2$

i) $P - 18 = 2P - 26$

j) $54 + 6M = 12 - M$

k) $8F - 6 = 4F - 26$

l) $11 - 25C = -22 - 14C$

m) $40 - 2D = -41 + 7D$

n) $8U + U - 17 = U + 47$

o) $35 + 2Y = 9Y - 14$

p) $19W + 16 = 7W - 8$

q) $X + 8 = 26$

r) $\dfrac{K}{2} + 4 = K - 2$

s) $19 = X - 3$

t) $64 = 4X$

u) $29 - 2T = 2 + T$ v) $-2 + Y = 17$

w) $-23 + R = 1$ x) $1N - 7 = \dfrac{N}{4} - 1$

y) $\dfrac{4H}{2} - H = -23 + 21$ z) $5 - 4W = -9 + 3W$

aa) $-7X - 13 = 7X + 1$

Teaching **LESSON # 25**

Fluency/Work Fast

Now that you have shown that you know how to solve multistep equations with transformations by simplifying variables across the equal sign, let's see how many accurate answers you can give in a 2-minute timed quiz. The problems in this quiz are all different, so read each problem carefully. We will start with this one. *(Point to any problem on the sheet.)* Once you give an answer, do not stop; go to the next question on the sheet to the right, or return to the next line below. Answer every question. If you skip a question, that counts as incorrect. If you happen to come to the last problem on the sheet, go to the top problem on the paper and do not stop. *(Run finger across and down the lines of problems to read like a paragraph.)* I will stop you 2 minutes after I say go.

This sheet can be used repeatedly for generalization and maintenance of skills.

Ready? Go.

Student   **LESSON # 26**

Graphical Representation

a) $Y = 2X + 5$

Circle the graph of the equation that matches the equation above.

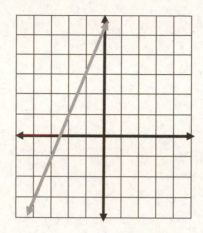   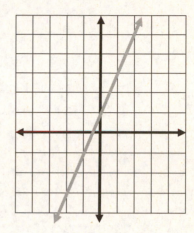

b) $2Y + \frac{1}{2}X + 3 = 2X$

Circle the graph of the equation that matches the equation above.

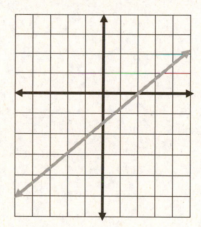   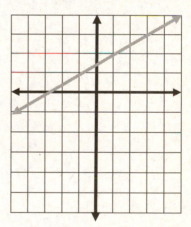

c) $3X + 5Y + 3 = -2X + 18$

Draw this equation on the graph below.

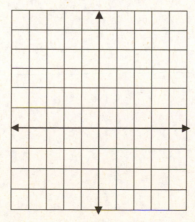

Teaching **LESSON # 26**

Graphical Representation

One reason we learned how to solve so many different types of variable equations is to prepare for graphing. Let's use this opportunity to transition our equation-solving skill to graphing on a coordinate plane.

You will solve each equation for Y, and then we will select which graph matches the equation.

Teach slope and intercept to help students choose which equation matches the equation.

Ready? Go.

Answer Key

▣ PRETEST

Section A
    a) $20U + 1W$ b) $-2P - 5$ c) $-$ or 0 d) $4B - 12$

Section B
    a) $F = 12$ b) $C = -11/3$ or $-3\frac{2}{3}$

    c) $X = 28/3$ or $9\frac{1}{3}$ d) $K = 42$

Section C
    a) $K = 4$ b) $P = 40$ c) $M = 5$ d) $D = -29$

Section D
    a) $Y = -1$ b) $N = 4$ c) $K = 2$ d) $F = 4$

Section E
    a) $F = 7$ b) $C = 3$ c) $N = 4$ d) $P = 20/3$ or $6\frac{2}{3}$

▣ POSTTEST

Section A
    a) $24U + 1G$ b) $-2N - 5$ c) $1Y - 5$ d) $4H - 12$

Section B
    a) $V = 20$ b) $C = -11/2$ or $-5\frac{1}{2}$

    c) $W = 28/3$ or $9\frac{1}{3}$ d) $B = 42$

Section C
    a) $R = 4$ b) $A = 40$ c) $T = 5$ d) $W = 1$

Section D
    a) $G = -1$ b) $Y = 4$ c) $P = 2$ d) $X = 4$

Section E
    a) $A = 7$ b) $N = 3$ c) $X = 4$ d) $K = 20/3$ or $6\frac{2}{3}$

LEARNING SHEETS

1. a) 3N + 2
   b) X − 3
   c) 4Y + 2
   d) 5
   e) 1/2N + 1
   f) 10 − 5x
   g) 2N + 6
   h) 2N + 7
   i) 5Y + 4
   j) −3X + 3
   k) 9 + 2Y
   l) 2N + 8

2. a) 2N − 1X + 12
   b) 3H − 5N − 2
   c) 5N − 2/3X − 7
   d) +2
   e) 7 − 3X + 1Y
   f) −4 + 5T
   g) 9U + 1W
   h) 3P + 11
   i) −1X + 4Y + 14
   j) 6W + 13
   k) 4B + 4L + 4
   l) 2F + 3X + 1W

3. a) 8 − 3F + 6X
   b) 7X + 7
   c) 1N + 4K + 2W
   d) 5X + 6
   e) 7/H + 3P − 1K − 1/2
   f) −10N + 15 + 1C
   g) 20U + 1W
   h) −2P − 5
   i) 4W + 8
   j) 2W + 6
   k) 20X + 14
   l) 2B + 2W − 2
   m) 6R or 6X when X or R represents red

4. a) −2X + 12K + 5
   b) 3W + 18 − 18G
   c) −2Y + 4Z + 13
   d) 7A
   e) 5Y + 4
   f) 8V − 5T − 3
   g) 0 or −
   h) 4B − 12
   i) −5M + 1R
   j) 21X + 14
   k) 8W + 15B
   l) 2P + 1L; P = 4(30) and L = 20; Total = 260 cars

5. a) −2Y + 15
   b) 12 cm − 10 in
   c) −2X + 18
   d) −1B
   e) −5M + 1R
   f) 4N + 18 + 16X
   g) 15R + 5
   h) 3Y − 5X + 5Z − 3
   i) 6H + 3
   j) −4F + 2G
   k) 18 + 13X
   l) 21N + 3 − 4R
   m) 31 − 9K − 1W
   n) 3X + 5
   o) 5Y + 4
   p) 20M + 3KM + 8

6. a) 1X = 3
   b) 1X = −2
   c) 1N = 4
   d) 1Y = 12
   e) 1Y = −2
   f) 1N = 8
   g) 1X = 9
   h) 1N = 6
   i) 1Y = 5
   j) 1X = 14
   k) 1N = 3
   l) 1Y = −3
   m) a. 3X = 15 b. 1X = 5
   n) a. 4N = 12 b. 1N = $3

7. a) 1T = −7
   b) 1Y = 3
   c) 1X = 18
   d) 1C = 3
   e) 1H = 2
   f) 1W = 12
   g) 1F = −2
   h) 1X = 15
   i) 1P = 4
   j) 1T = −7
   k) 1Y = 5
   l) 1X = −5
   m) 1N = −15
   n) 1P = 8
   o) a. C/5 = 2 b. C = 10

8. a) 1Y = 4
   b) 1W = 22
   c) 1P = −3
   d) 1X = 10
   e) 1P = −8
   f) 1M = −1
   g) 1F = 12
   h) 1C = −11
   i) 1D = 81
   j) 1U = 40
   k) 1Y = 7
   l) 1W = −2
   m) 5B = 25; B = 5

9. a) 1T = 12/5 or 2⅖
   b) M = 21/2 or 10½
   c) 1X = 30
   d) 1C = −33/5 or −6⅗
   e) 1X = 28/3 or 9⅓
   f) K = 42
   g) 1X = 19/3 or 6⅓
   h) 1X = 16

    i) $1Y = -17/2$ or $-8\frac{1}{2}$ j) $1R = 4/3$ or $1\frac{1}{3}$

    k) $1N = 15/2$ or $7\frac{1}{2}$ l) $1P = 9/2$ or $4\frac{1}{2}$

    m) $20 - P = 3; P = 17$ n) $11T = 33; T = 3$

10. a) $X = -9$ b) $X = 10$ c) $X = 6$

     d) $X = 4$ e) $Y = -9$ f) $Y = 3$

     g) $Y = 15$ h) $Y = 7\frac{1}{2}$ i) $N = -4$

     j) $N = 4$ k) $N = 32$ l) $N = -1/8$

     m) $P = 8$ n) $P = 10$ o) $P = -9$

     p) $P = -2$

11. a) $1N = 3$ b) $1X = 9$ c) $1N = 2$

     d) $1Y = 8/3$ or $2\frac{2}{3}$ e) $1X = 9$ f) $1N = 1/2$

     g) $1Y = 2$ h) $1X = 2$ i) $1X = 6$

     j) $1Y = 3\frac{1}{2}$ k) $1Y = 2$ l) $1N = 2$

     m) $18 = 3P; P = 6$ n) $15 - X = 2; X = 13$

12. a) $1N = 7$ b) $1X = 8\frac{1}{2}$ c) $1Y = 20$

     d) $1Y = 2$ e) $1C = 3$ f) $1W = 2\frac{2}{5}$

     g) $1Y = 5$ h) $1M = 6$ i) $1Y = -3$

     j) $1X = 2$ k) $1W = 7$ l) $1N = 7\frac{1}{2}$

     m) $10 - S = 7; 1S = 13$ n) $8/N = 2; 1N = 4$

13. a) $1P = 9$ b) $1H = 3$ c) $1M = 4$

     d) $1C = -48$ e) $1X = -26$ f) $1X = 10$

     g) $1N = 4$ h) $1R = 12$ i) $1Y = -1$

     j) $1Y = 6$ k) $1K = 4$ l) $1P = 40$

     m) $10/T = 9; 1T = 10$ n) $R - 10 = 28; 1R = 38$

14. a) $1A = -5$ b) $1X = 8$ c) $1W = 15$

     d) $1H = -3/2$ or $-1\frac{1}{2}$ e) $1Y = 10$

     f) $1J = -6$ g) $1G = 1$ h) $1Y = 4$

     i) $1Y = 1/2$ j) $1X = 4$ k) $1F = 6$

     l) $1N = -36$ m) $1M = 5$ n) $1D = -20$

     o) $1D = 5$ p) $10 - M = 10; 1M = 20$

15. Level 1:

     a) $1X = 13$ b) $1X = 9$ c) $1X = -1$

     d) $1X = 48$ e) $1X = -9$ f) $1X = 5$

     g) $1Y = 13$ h) $1Y = 3$ i) $1Y = 12$

     j) $1Y = 19$ k) $1Y = -27$ l) $1Y = 12$

     m) $1W = 27$ n) $1W = 16$ o) $1W = 42$

     p) $1W = 26$ q) $1W = 40$ r) $1W = 42$

     s) $1N = 18$ t) $1N = 7$ u) $1N = 16$

     v) $1N = 19$ w) $1N = 49$ x) $1N = -22$

     y) $1P = 30$ z) $1P = 4$ aa) $1P = 9$

     bb) $1P = -11$ cc) $1P = 32$ dd) $1P = 5$

15. Level 2:

     a) $1Y = 13$ b) $1Y = 4$ c) $1Y = 3$

     d) $1Y = 7$ e) $1Y = -1\frac{1}{3}$ f) $1Y = -36$

g) 1M = 10   h) 1M = 9   i) 1M = −2

j) 1M = 4⅘   k) 1M = 4   l) 1M = 21

m) 1W = 10   n) 1W = −1/5   o) 1W = 0

p) 1W = 12   q) 1W = 9   r) 1W = −1/3

s) 1X = 1   t) 1X = 8¾   u) 1X = 3

v) 1X = −24   w) 1X = −6   x) 1X = 6

y) 1U = 14⅔   z) 1U = 5   aa) 1U = 9

16. a) 1N = 8   b) 1X = −2   c) 1X = 7½

d) 1Y = 1   e) 1X = −8   f) 1N = 5

g) 1Y = 3   h) 1N = 3   i) 1Y = −7

j) 1X = −3   k) 1N = 4   l) 1Y = 4

m) E + 3E = $12; 1E = $3 (1E = $3,000)

n) 3B + 1B = 16 volts; 1B = 4 volts

17. a) 1N = −2   b) 1H = 9½   c) 1Y = −17

d) 1T = 8   e) 1C = 4   f) 1W = −9

g) 1G = 1   h) 1W = 16   i) 1P = −2

j) 1X = 4   k) 1P = 2   l) 1Y = 3

m) 2P + 5P = $14; 1P = $2   n) 3G + 2G = $15 + $5; 1G = $4

18. a) 1Y = −9   b) 1M = 2   c) 1W = −12

d) 1C = 3   e) 1W = 3   f) 1X = 5

g) 1W = 7   h) 1Y = 8   i) 1Y = −1

j) 1N = 7   k) 1V = 1   l) 1K = 5

m) X + 2X = 15; sister = $5 and mom = $10

n) 5B + 2B = 5(7); 1B = 5

19. a) 1P = 5⅓   b) 1C = 3   c) 1W = 3

d) 1M = 1⅓   e) 1W = 2¼   f) 1P = 6

g) 1N = 4⅜   h) 1Y = 2   i) 1K = 2

j) 1F = 4   k) 1V = 4   l) 1K = 40

m) $40/4 + X = $56; 1X = $16   n) ISOLATE − list steps

20. a) 1R = 4   b) 1R = 6   c) 1R = 5

d) 1R = 1   e) 1X = 2   f) 1X = 9

g) 1X = −12   h) 1X = 9   i) 1N = 2

j) 1N = 18   k) 1V = 1   l) 1V = 7

m) 1V = 2   n) 1V = 10   o) 1Y = 10

p) 1Y = 1   q) 1Y = 1   r) 1Y = 8

21. a) 1X = −2   b) 1X = 4   c) 1N = 3

d) 1Y = 2   e) 1Y = 3   f) 1N = −3

g) 1X = 3   h) 1N = 4   i) 1Y = 7

j) 1X = 7   k) 1Y = 9   l) 1X = 2

m) 20 + X = 2X; 1X = 20   n) 12 − Y = Y; 1Y = 6

22. a) 1T = −4   b) 1Y = 7   c) 1X = 4

d) 1C = 6   e) 1H = 5   f) 1W = 1

g) 1F = −11   h) 1V = 7   i) 1P = −2

j) 1T = 5   k) 1Y = 4   l) 1X = 2

m) N + 15 + 2N + 3; 1N = 12

23. a) 1Y = −10   b) 1K = 13   c) 1W = 2

d) 1X = −1   e) 1P = −20   f) 1M = 5

g) 1F = 8   h) 1C = 3   i) 1D = 3

j) 1U = 3   k) 1Y = 5   l) 1W = −2

m) 1X + 12 = 2X + 0; 1X = 12

24. a) 1T = −8   b) 1P = 6⅔   c) 1X = 7

d) 1M = 9   e) 1X = 6   f) 1K = −21

g) 1X = 8   h) 1X = 15   i) 1Y = 7

j) 1R = 4   k) 1N = 4   l) 1C = 5

m) 1B = −4   n) 1N = 1/2

o) 3hX/2g = 6h; X = 4g, when h = hours and g = gallons

25. a) 1Y = 9   b) 1X = −11   c) 1Y = 9

d) 1X = −2   e) 1P = −2   f) 1P = −9

g) 1Y = 7   h) 1X = 5   i) 1P = 8

j) 1M = −7   k) 1F = −4   l) 1C = 3

m) 1D = 9   n) 1U = 8   o) 1Y = 7

p) 1W = −2   q) 1X = 18   r) 1K = 12

s) 1X = 22   t) 1X = 16   u) 1T = −9

v) 1Y = 19   w) 1R = 24   x) 1N = 8

y) 1H = −2   z) 1W = 2   aa) 1X = −1

26. a) Left graph   b) Left graph

c)

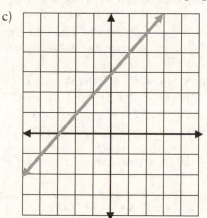

References

Butler, F. M., Miller, S. P., Crehan, K., Babbit, B., & Pierce, T. (2003). Fraction instruction for students with mathematics disabilities: Comparing two teaching sequences. *Learning Disabilities Research & Practice, 18*(2), 99–111.

Cawley, J. F., & Miller, J. H. (1989). Crosssectional comparison of the mathematical performance of children with learning disabilities: Are we on the right track toward comprehensive programming? *Journal of Learning Disabilities, 23*, 250–254, 259.

Gagnon, J. G., & Maccini, P. (2007). Teacher–reported use of empirically validated standards-based instructional approaches in secondary mathematics. *Remedial and Special Education, 28*(1), 43–56.

Hutchinson, N. L. (1993). Second invited response: Students with disabilities and mathematics education reform—Let the dialog begin. *Remedial and Special Education, 14*(6), 20–23.

Jordan, L., Miller, M. D., & Mercer, C. D. (1999). The effects of concrete to semi–concrete to abstract instruction in the acquisition and retention of fraction concepts and skills. *Learning Disabilities: A Multidisciplinary Journal, 9*, 115–122.

Kieran (1992) The learning and teaching of school algebra. In D. Grouws (Ed.), *Handbook of research on mathematics teaching and learning* (pp. 390–419). New York: Macmillan.

Lacampagne, C. B. (1995). Conceptual framework for the algebra initiative of the National Institute on Student Achievement, Curriculum, and Assessment. In C. B. Lacampagne, W. Blair, & J. Kaput, (Eds.), The *algebra initiative colloquium* (2nd ed, pp. 237–242). Washington, DC: U.S. Department of Education, Office of Educational Research and Improvement, and National Institute on Student Achievement, Curriculum, and Assessment.

Maccini, P., & Hughes, C. A. (2000). Effects of a problem–solving strategy on the introductory algebra performance of secondary students with learning disabilities. *Learning Disabilities Research & Practice, 15*, 10–21.

Maccini, P., McNaughton, D., & Ruhl, K. L. (1999). Algebra instruction for students with learning disabilities: Implications from a research review. *Learning Disability Quarterly, 22*, 113–126.

Maccini, P., Mulcahy, C. A., & Wilson, M. G. (2007). A follow–up of mathematics interventions for secondary students with learning disabilities. *Learning Disabilities Research & Practice, 22*(1), 58–74.

Miles, D. D., & Forcht, J. P. (1995). Mathematics strategies for secondary students with learning disabilities or mathematics deficiencies: A cognitive strategy approach. *Intervention in School & Clinic, 31*(2), 91–96.

National Mathematics Advisory Panel. (2008). *Foundations for success: The final report of the national mathematics advisory report*. Washington, DC: U.S. Department of Education. Retrieved January 8, 2010, from http://www.ed.gov/MathPanel.

Riccomini, P. J., & Witzel, B. S. (2010). *Response to intervention in math*. Thousand Oaks, CA: Corwin Press.

Sanders, S., Riccomini, P. J., & Witzel, B. S. (2005). The algebra readiness of high school students in South Carolina: Implications for middle school math teachers. *South Carolina Middle School Journal, 13*, 45–47.

Witzel, B. (2005). Using CRA to teach algebra to students with math difficulties in inclusive settings. *Learning Disabilities: A Contemporary Journal, 3*(2), 49–60.

Witzel, B. S., Mercer, C. D., & Miller, M. D. (2003). Teaching algebra to students with learning difficulties: An investigation of an explicit instruction model. *Learning Disabilities Research & Practice, 18*(2), 121–131.

Witzel, B. S., & Riccomini, P. J. (2009). *Computations of integers: Math intervention for elementary and middle grades*. Upper Saddle River, NJ: Pearson.

Appendix—Learning Sheets and Assessments

Pretest

Name: _____

Section A—Reducing expressions

a) $4U(5) - W + 2W$ b) $-3P + 7 + P - 12$

c) $8 - 2(X + 4) + 2X$ d) $8A + 4B - 4(2A) - 12$

Section B—One-step inverse operations

a) $16 = \dfrac{4F}{6}$ b) $11 = -3C$

c) $3X = 28$ d) $\dfrac{K}{7} = 6$

Section C—Two+-step inverse operations

a) $\dfrac{44}{K} = 11$ b) $2 + \dfrac{1P}{2} = 22$

c) $2 = \dfrac{2M}{5}$ d) $19 = -10 - D$

Section D—Simplifying and solving equations

a) $9 = -Y - 8Y$ b) $12N - 5N - 5 = 13 + 10$

c) $\dfrac{10}{K} = \dfrac{35}{7}$ d) $10F - F + 1F - 4 = 36$

Section E—Transformational equations

a) $8F - 16 = 2F + 26$ b) $11 - 5C = -22 + 6C$

c) $2N - 8 = \dfrac{1N}{2} - 2$ d) $\dfrac{P}{2} + 2 = 2P - 8$

Posttest

Name: _____

Section A—Reducing expressions

a) $3U(8) - G + 2G$

b) $-3N + 7 + N - 12$

c) $7 - 3(Y + 4) + 2Y$

d) $8C + 4H - 4(2C) - 12$

Section B—One-step inverse operations

a) $10 = \dfrac{3V}{6}$

b) $11 = -2X$

c) $3W = 28$

d) $\dfrac{B}{7} = 6$

Section C—Two+-step inverse operations

a) $\dfrac{44}{R} = 11$

b) $2 + \dfrac{1A}{2} = 22$

c) $2 = \dfrac{2T}{5}$

d) $-9 = -10 + W$

Section D—Simplifying and solving equations

a) $9 = -G - 8G$

b) $12Y - 5Y - 5 = 13 + 10$

c) $\dfrac{10}{P} = \dfrac{35}{7}$

d) $10X - X + 1X - 4 = 36$

Section E—Transformational equations

a) $8A - 16 = 2A + 26$

b) $11 - 5N = -22 + 6N$

c) $2X - 8 = \dfrac{1X}{2} - 2$

d) $\dfrac{1K}{2} + 2 = 2K - 8$

LESSON # 1

Concrete/Hands-on: Simplifying by Combining Like Terms

Describe/Model

a) $1N + 7 + 2N - 5$ b) $X + 3 - 6$

Guided Practice

c) $3Y + Y + 2$ d) $-N + N + 5$

e) $\dfrac{1N}{2} - 4 + 5$ f) $10 - 2X - 3X$

Independent Practice

g) $N + N + 6$ h) $5 + 2N + 2$

i) $3Y + 4 + 2Y$ j) $-X - 2X + 3$

Problem Solving

k) While cleaning up your room, you find 3 books (3) and (+) two bags of books (2Y) under your bed. Then, on the floor you see 6 more books (+6). Set up the simplest expression and show how many books you found.

l) In PE, the teacher throws out 5 balls (5), 2 sacks of balls (2N), and then 3 more balls (+3). Set up the simplest equation and show how many balls there were in PE.

LESSON # 2

Representations/Pictures

Describe/Model

a) $2N - 2X + 12 + X$ b) $3H - 5N - 2$

Guided Practice

c) $4N - \dfrac{2X}{3} + N - 7$ d) $T - 3T + 2T + 2$

e) $4 - 3X + 3 + Y$ f) $-6 + T + 4T + 2$

Independent Practice

g) $4U + 5U - W + 2W$ h) $6P + 4 - 3P + 7$

i) $3X + 4Y + 14 - 4X$ j) $2L + 6W - 2L + 13$

Problem Solving

k) You can carry only so many books. One teacher gives you 2 big books (2B) and 4 small books (4L) along with 4 pieces of paper (4) to carry. Your next teacher gives you 2 more big books (2B) to carry home. Set up the simplest expression to show how many books and pieces of paper you have to carry.

l) You are helping make a cake and icing. The cake takes 2 cups of flour (2F) and 1 cup of sugar (1X). The icing takes 2 cups of sugar (2X) and 1 cup of water (1W). What are the total *ingredients*? Set up the simplest expression to solve the problem.

LESSON # 3

Abstract

Describe/Model

a) $8 - 3F + 2(3X)$

b) $3(X + 2) + X + 1$

Guided Practice

c) $-N + 4K + 2W + 2N$

d) $\dfrac{24Z}{6} + 6 + Z$

e) $\dfrac{7}{H} + 3P - \dfrac{1}{2} - K$

f) $-5N + 5 - 5N + 10 + C$

Independent Practice

g) $4U(5) - W + 2W$

h) $-3P + 7 + P - 12$

i) $-1\dfrac{12W}{3} + 4 - 12$

j) $2W + 6 - 2K + 2K$

k) $6X(4) + 14 - 4X$

l) $2B - 2W - 12 + 10$

Problem Solving

m) Your uncle brought 4 red presents and 2 blue presents to the party. Your little brother then took two blue presents. Aunt Patty brought 2 more red presents. Set up the expression to figure out how many presents were left.

n) The football team passed the ball for 5 yards and then ran for 4 yards. They passed for 10 yards more and then ran for a loss of 2 yards. Set up the expression to show how many yards were gained by the team through running and passing.

LESSON # 4

Abstract

Describe/Model

a) $5X + 12K - 7X + 5$ b) $3W + 6(3 - G)$

Guided Practice

c) $Y + 4Z + 5 - 3Y + 8$ d) $\frac{1}{2}(8A + 4A) + 5A$

Independent Mixed Practice

e) $3Y + 4 + 2Y$ f) $3V - 5T + 5V - 3$

g) $8 - 2(X + 4) + 2X$ h) $8A + 4B - 4(2A) - 12$

i) $9M - 6R + 7(R - 2M)$ j) $X + 18 + 20X - 4$

Problem Solving

k) To build a house you need supplies. You bring 3 bundles of wood and 5 pallets of bricks. The foreman brings an additional 10 pallets of bricks and 5 bundles of wood. Set up a simple expression to show what was brought.

l) A parking company wants to estimate their income for the day. They own 2 parking garages and 1 parking lot. Each parking garage has 4 floors where there are 30 cars per floor. The parking lot has 20 cars. Set up a simple expression to help the company calculate the total income. Explain your rationale.

LESSON # 5

Fluency/Work Fast

a) $6Y + 14 - 8Y + 1$

b) $3CM - 7IN + 9CM - 3IN$

c) $-2(X + 1) + 20$

d) $3A + 3A - 3A(2) - B$

e) $9M - 6R + 7(R - 2M)$

f) $4N + 18 + 20X - 4X$

g) $4R + 12R + 5 - R$

h) $3Y - 5X + 5Z - 3$

i) $2H + 2(H + H) + 3$

j) $8F + 4G - 2G - 12F$

k) $5 + 13(X + 1)$

l) $N + 3 + 20N - 4R$

m) $19 - 9K + 12 - W$

n) $1/3(6X + 15) + X$

o) $3Y + 4 + 2Y$

p) $2DM + 5KM + 8 - 2KM$

LESSON # 6

Concrete/Hands-on: Solving Inverse Operations (One-Step Equations)

Describe/Model

a) $1X = 3$

b) $-8 = 4X$

c) $\dfrac{N}{2} = 2$

d) $\dfrac{1Y}{3} = 4$

Guided Practice

e) $6 = -3Y$

f) $\dfrac{N}{4} = 2$

g) $3 = \dfrac{1X}{3}$

h) $2N = 12$

Independent Practice

i) $10 = 2Y$

j) $7 = \dfrac{X}{2}$

k) $3N = 9$

l) $\dfrac{Y}{3} = -1$

Problem Solving

m) In a basketball game, three players (3X) scored (=) 15 points together. What is the average amount of points that each scored?

1. Set up the equation.
2. Answer the equation.

n) Frank sold cell phones. If he sold 4 cell phones (4N) he made (=) $12. How much did he make per cell phone? Let N = cost per phone.

1. Set up the equation.
2. Answer the equation

LESSON # 7

Representational/Pictures (One-Step Equations)

Describe/Model

    a) $7 = -T$ b) $12 = 4Y$

    c) $3 = \dfrac{X}{6}$ d) $\dfrac{2C}{3} = 2$

Guided Practice

    e) $2 = H$ f) $\dfrac{W}{4} = 3$

    g) $-3F = 6$ h) $5 = \dfrac{1X}{3}$

Independent Practice

    i) $4P = 16$ j) $14 = -2T$

    k) $25 = 5Y$ l) $10 = -2X$

    m) $-3 = \dfrac{N}{5}$ n) $\dfrac{1P}{2} = 4$

Problem Solving

    o) Carl (C) had a large number of chocolates. He split (÷) them among 5 friends. After he split them (=), each friend had 2 chocolates. How many did he have total? Set up the equation and solve.

LESSON # 8

Abstract

Describe/Model

a) $8 = -2Y$

b) $\dfrac{2W}{4} = 11$

Guided Practice

c) $-27 = 9P$

d) $6 = \dfrac{3X}{5}$

Independent Practice

e) $P = -8$

f) $-14 = 14M$

g) $16 = \dfrac{4F}{6}$

h) $11 = -C$

i) $81 = \dfrac{9D}{9}$

j) $8 = \dfrac{U}{5}$

k) $63 = 9Y$

l) $8 = -4W$

Problem Solving

m) Al's backpack could carry 5 books. How many backpacks would Al need to carry 25 books? Set up the equation and solve.

LESSON # 9

Abstract II

Describe/Model

a) $T5 = 12$

b) $7 = \dfrac{2M}{3}$

Guided Practice

c) $12 = \dfrac{2X}{5}$

d) $5C = -33$

Independent Practice

e) $3X = 28$

f) $\dfrac{K}{7} = 6$

g) $19 = X3$

h) $64 = 4X$

i) $2Y = -17$

j) $6R = 8$

k) $5 = \dfrac{2N}{3}$

l) $\dfrac{4P}{6} = 3$

Problem Solving

m) Jose had 20 pencils and gave some away. He had 3 left. How many did he give away? Set up the equation and solve.

n) There are 11 players per team and many teams. If there are 33 players, how many teams are there? Set up the equation and solve.

LESSON # 10

Fluency/Work Fast)

a) $3X = -27$

b) $\dfrac{X}{2} = 5$

c) $18 = X3$

d) $24 = 6X$

e) $-2Y = 18$

f) $3Y = 9$

g) $5 = \dfrac{1Y}{3}$

h) $\dfrac{2Y}{5} = 3$

i) $5N = -20$

j) $12 = 3N$

k) $8 = \dfrac{N}{4}$

l) $1 = -8N$

m) $6 = \dfrac{3P}{4}$

n) $2 = \dfrac{P}{5}$

o) $81 = -9P$

p) $16 = -8P$

LESSON # 11

Concrete/Hands-on (Two-Step Equations)

Describe/Model

a) $1N + 5 = 8$　　　b) $4 = X - 5$

c) $2N + 3 = 7$　　　d) $8 = 0 + 3Y$

Guided Practice

e) $X - 3 = 5$　　　f) $7 + 2N = 8$

g) $11 = 3 + 4Y$　　　h) $9 = 3X + 3$

Independent Practice

i) $X - 4 = 2$　　　j) $8 = 2Y + 1$

k) $8 = 2Y + 4$　　　l) $1 = 3N - 5$

Problem Solving

m) A cake has 18 pieces. The pieces were divided among a few people. In the end (=), each person received 3 pieces of cake. How many people were there? Set up the equation and solve for the variable.

n) The shop owner earned $15. She gives you some for helping her (+X). You see (=) she kept $2. How much money does she give you? Set up the equation and solve for the variable.

LESSON # 12

Representational/Pictures (Two-Step Equations)

Describe/Model

a) $10 - N = 3$
b) $12 = -5 + 2X$

c) $\dfrac{Y}{5} + 1 = 5$
d) $6 = \dfrac{12}{Y}$

Guided Practice

e) $-4 = 8 - 4C$
f) $5W - 2 = 10$

g) $5 = \dfrac{25}{Y}$
h) $\dfrac{2M}{3} = 4$

Independent Practice

i) $9 = -2Y + 3$
j) $6 - 4X = -2$

k) $\dfrac{14}{W} = 2$
l) $\dfrac{2N}{3} = 5$

Problem Solving

m) You pull out $20 to pay for you haircut. You don't know how much the haircut costs. After you hand the money over (=), the barber hands you $7 change. How much did the haircut cost?

n) Mr. W. had to divide 8 books among some students (N). Each student had 2 books. How many students were there? Set up the equation and solve.

LESSON # 13

Abstract

Describe/Model

a) $\dfrac{72}{P} = 8$

b) $8 = 14 - H2$

Guided Practice

c) $\dfrac{36}{M} = 8$

d) $9 = -7 - \dfrac{1C}{3}$

Independent Practice

e) $-13 - X = 13$

f) $-2X + 13 = -7$

g) $8 = \dfrac{32}{N}$

h) $\dfrac{2R}{4} = 6$

i) $19 = -Y + 18$

j) $9 = \dfrac{54}{Y}$

k) $\dfrac{44}{K} = 11$

l) $2 + \dfrac{1P}{2} = 22$

Problem Solving

m) 90 of Suzie's closest friends came to her birthday party. She divides them into several teams to play football. If each team has 9 people, how many teams are there? Set up the equation and solve.

n) Last year it rained an unknown amount. It rained 10 inches less this year. This year it rained 28 inches. How many inches did it rain last year? Set the equation and solve.

LESSON # 14

Abstract II

Describe/Model

a) $52 = -4A + 32$ b) $\dfrac{54}{X} + 1 = 7$

Guided Practice

c) $\dfrac{2W}{5} = 6$ d) $17 = 14 - H2$

Independent Practice

e) $3 = \dfrac{30}{Y}$ f) $-4J - 8 = 16$

g) $23 = \dfrac{23}{G}$ h) $\dfrac{3Y}{2} = 6$

i) $9 = 2Y + 8$ j) $16 - X = 12$

k) $\dfrac{48}{F} = 8$ l) $2 - \dfrac{N}{6} = 8$

m) $2 = \dfrac{2M}{5}$ n) $19 = -1 - D$

Problem Solving

o) Mrs. Millionaire owned 10 cars and divided them among her daughters. If each daughter ended up with 2 cars, how many daughters were there?

p) Margie was loaned money by her mom, but she forgot how much. In her pocket she found a store receipt that said she spent $10 for a CD and had $10 change. How much did her mother loan her? Set up the equation and solve.

LESSON # 16

Concrete/Hands-on: Solving for a Variable When Like Variables Are on the Same Side

Describe/Model

a) $-N + 2N = 8$

b) $9 = -X - X + 5$

c) $10 + 5 = 2X - X + X$

d) $2Y + 1Y = 3$

Guided Practice

e) $5 = -X - 3$

f) $2N + 3 - N = 8$

g) $12 = 4Y - Y + 1Y$

h) $9 = N + 2N$

Independent Practice

i) $7 = -3Y + 2Y$

j) $-X - X - X = 9$

k) $8 = 2N - N + N$

l) $Y + 3Y = 16$

Problem Solving

m) 1 employee's (E) salary must be added (+) to another 3 employees' (3E) salaries. Their total (=) salaries are $12 (for 12,000). How much does each employee earn? Set up the equation and solve.

n) 3 batteries (3B) are added to the 1 battery (1B) in Jan's game controller. The total voltage of the batteries is (=) 16 volts. What is the voltage of each battery? Set up and solve the equation.

LESSON # 17

Representational/Pictures

Describe/Model

a) $9 + N + 2N = 3$ b) $15 = -4 + 3H - H$

c) $10 + 6 = 2Y - 3Y$ d) $12 = T5 - T + 4$

Guided Practice

e) $-4 = 8 - C(3)$ f) $-2W + W - 2 = 7$

g) $2G + G + G2 = 2 + 3$ h) $2W + W = 13 + 3$

Independent Practice

i) $P4 - 2P = -12 + 8$ j) $5X - X = 11 + 6 - 1$

k) $12 + 2 = 4P + 3P$ l) $12 = 7Y - Y5 + 6$

Problem Solving

m) Chuck brings home 2 paychecks from last week. He adds these to the previous 5 paychecks. He now has made $14 (in thousands). How much is each paycheck? Set up and solve the equation.

n) Marsha cleaned 3 garages on Saturday and 2 garages on Monday. She made $15 on Saturday and $5 on Monday. What is the average amount she earned for each garage cleaned? Set up the equation and solve.

LESSON # 18

Abstract

Describe/Model

a) $\dfrac{72}{8} = -4Y + Y3$

b) $12 - 6 = \dfrac{12}{M}$

Guided Practice

c) $36 + 12 = 12 - 2W - W$

d) $-3(5) = -2C - C3$

Independent Practice

e) $3W = \dfrac{54}{9} + 3$

f) $-X - 2X = -17 + 2$

g) $6W - 4(W) = \dfrac{36}{6} + 8$

h) $75 - 3 = 12Y - Y - Y - Y$

i) $9 = -Y - 8Y$

j) $12N - 5N - 5 = 13 + 10$

k) $\dfrac{4}{V} = 1 + 3$

l) $7K - 2K = 11(2) + 3$

Problem Solving

m) Your sister gave you money for your birthday. Your mom gave you 2 times as much as your sister. Together they gave you $15 total. How much did each person give you? Set up the equation and solve.

n) Mario sold 5 boxes of books to one man and 2 boxes of books to another. He sold a total of 5 times 7 books altogether. How many books total did he sell? Set up the equation and solve.

LESSON # 19
Abstract II

Describe/Model

a) $8P - 2P = 32$

b) $\dfrac{15}{C} = \dfrac{10}{2}$

Guided Practice

c) $\dfrac{42}{7W} = 2$

d) $2(8) = 3M + 9M$

Independent Practice

e) $7(W) - 3W = \dfrac{18}{2}$

f) $44 = 8P - 2P + 20$

g) $2N + 6(N) = 35$

h) $\dfrac{60}{5} = 5Y + Y$

i) $\dfrac{10}{K} = \dfrac{35}{7}$

j) $10F - F + 1F - 4 = 36$

k) $\dfrac{36}{6} = \dfrac{24}{V}$

l) $\dfrac{14X}{2} - 6X = 30 + 10$

Problem Solving

m) Eric paid $40 for the movies with his friends. He paid the extra cost for the popcorn and the drinks. The total cost was $56. How much did Eric spend on popcorn and drinks? Set up the equation and solve.

n) List the steps to solving for an unknown quantity.

LESSON # 20
Fluency/Work Fast

a) $6(R) - 3R = \dfrac{24}{2}$

b) $15 = 8R - 2R - 3$

c) $5R + 2(R) = 35$

d) $\dfrac{30}{5} = 2R + 4R$

e) $\dfrac{35}{7} + 3 = 4X$

f) $-2X - X = -17 + -10$

g) $2X - 3(X) = 20 - 8$

h) $80 + 1 = 12X - X - X - X$

i) $\dfrac{24}{6} = \dfrac{8}{N}$

j) $\dfrac{2N}{3} = 10 + 2$

k) $-9 = -4V - 5V$

l) $11 + 10 = 10V - 7V$

m) $\dfrac{12}{V} = 3 + 3$

n) $4V - 2V = 25 - 5$

o) $5Y + 5(Y) = 50$

p) $\dfrac{30}{6} = 5Y$

q) $\dfrac{8}{Y} = \dfrac{40}{5}$

r) $3Y - 6Y = -24$

LESSON # 21

Concrete/Hands-on: Solving for a Variable When Like Variables Are on Opposite Sides

Describe/Model

a) $X = 3X + 4$

b) $3X - 8 = X$

c) $1N = 4N - 9$

d) $3Y = 10 - 2Y$

Guided Practice

e) $Y = 2Y - 3$

f) $6 + N = -N$

g) $3X = 12 - X$

h) $N = -N + 8$

Independent Practice

i) $14 - Y = Y$

j) $X + 7 = 2X$

k) $2Y + 9 = 3Y$

l) $X = 6 - 2X$

Problem Solving

m) Tom had $20 (20) added (+) to his usual pay (X). He now has (=) 2 times what he is normally paid (2X). What is his normal pay? Set up the equation and solve.

n) Carrie had $12 (12). Some money was taken away (−Y). She ended up (=) with the same amount that was taken away from her (Y). Set up the equation and solve.

LESSON # 22

Representational/Pictures

Describe/Model

a) $T - 8 = 3T$ b) $6 - Y = Y - 8$

c) $3 - 3X = X - 9$ d) $5C - C = C + 18$

Guided Practice

e) $2 + H = -13 + 4H$ f) $7W = 3 + 4W$

g) $-3 + F = 2F + 8$ h) $16 + V = 3V + 2$

Independent Practice

i) $-P - 7 = 5 + 5P$ j) $12 - 2T = -3 + T$

k) $5 + Y = 3Y - 3$ l) $8 + 2X = 5X + 2$

Problem Solving

m) The price of 1 CD (N) plus $15 (+15) is (=) the same as 2 CDs (2N) plus $3. How much does 1 CD cost? Set up the equation and solve.

LESSON # 23

Abstract

Describe/Model

a) $8 + 4Y = Y - 22$ b) $2K + 3K = 11 + 2 + 4K$

Guided Practice

c) $5 - 4W = -9 + 3W$ d) $-7X - 13 = 7X + 1$

Independent Practice

e) $P - 18 = 2P + 2$ f) $-14 + 6M = 11 + M$

g) $8F - 16 = 2F + 26$ h) $11 - 5C = -22 + 6C$

i) $15 - 2D = -12 + 7D$ j) $8U + U - 17 = U + 7$

k) $27 + 2Y = 7Y + 2$ l) $19W + 16 = 7W - 8$

Problem Solving

m) Two brothers were given an equal amount of money and bought equally priced games. Brandon bought one game for himself and had $12 left. Taylor bought 2 games and had $0 left. Since both brothers had the same amount of money, how much did each video game cost? Set up the equation and solve.

LESSON # 24

Abstract II

Describe/Model

a) $\dfrac{T}{2} - 3 = T + 1$　　　b) $\dfrac{P}{2} + 2 = 2P - 8$

Guided Practice

c) $13 - X = \dfrac{6X}{3} - 8$　　d) $-5 + M = \dfrac{1M}{3} + 1$

Independent Practice

e) $X + 8 = 26 - 2X$　　f) $\dfrac{K}{7} + 5 = 2$

g) $21 - X = 2X - 3$　　h) $30 + X = 3X$

i) $-4 + Y + 2Y = 17$　　j) $-23 + 6R = 1$

k) $2N - 8 = \dfrac{1N}{2} - 2$　　l) $15C - 12 = 13 + 10C$

m) $-3B - 8 = B + 8$　　n) $2N + N + 12 = 3 + N + 10$

Problem Solving

o) You fill a lawnmower with an unknown number of gallons of gas. You know it goes for about 3/2 hours per gallon. If the mower runs for 6 hours until it is empty, how many gallons does it hold?

LESSON # 25

Fluency/Work Fast

a) $18 - Y = Y$ b) $X - 11 = 2X$

c) $2Y + 9 = 3Y$ d) $X = 6 - 2X$

e) $-P - 7 = 13 + 9P$ f) $\dfrac{P}{5} + 2 = 3P + 12$

g) $25 + Y = 5Y - 3$ h) $13 + 2X = 5X - 2$

i) $P - 18 = 2P - 26$ j) $54 + 6M = 12 - M$

k) $8F - 6 = 4F - 26$ l) $11 - 25C = -22 - 14C$

m) $40 - 2D = -41 + 7D$ n) $8U + U - 17 = U + 47$

o) $35 + 2Y = 9Y - 14$ p) $19W + 16 = 7W - 8$

q) $X + 8 = 26$ r) $\dfrac{K}{2} + 4 = K - 2$

s) $19 = X - 3$ t) $64 = 4X$

u) $29 - 2T = 2 + T$ v) $-2 + Y = 17$

w) $-23 + R = 1$ x) $1N - 7 = \dfrac{N}{4} - 1$

y) $\dfrac{4H}{2} - H = -23 + 21$ z) $5 - 4W = -9 + 3W$

aa) $-7X - 13 = 7X + 1$

LESSON # 26

Graphical Representation

a) $Y = 2X + 5$

Circle the graph of the equation that matches the equation above.

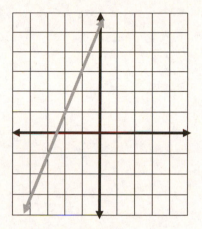 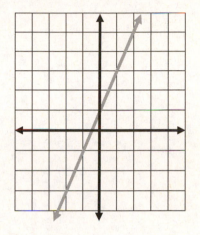

b) $2Y + \frac{1}{2}X + 3 = 2X$

Circle the graph of the equation that matches the equation above.

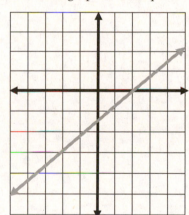 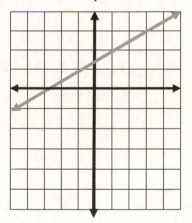

c) $3X + 5Y + 3 = -2X + 18$

Draw this equation on the graph below.

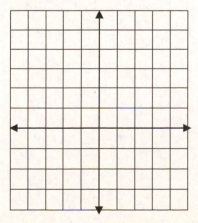

Appendix—Materials

Summary Chart for Concrete to Representation to Abstract Materials

Material Sample	Overhead Samples	Desktop Samples	Pictorial Representations	Abstract Notation
Digit	/	/	/	1–9
Ten	|	|	|	10
Group	(cup)	(cup)	◯ or (rounded square)	0 or above may be an assumed 1
Divisor line	▭	▭	——	—
Equal sign	)	}	)	=
Positive or Addition Symbol	⊕	⊞	+	+
Negative or Subtraction Symbol	⊖	⊟	–	–

Multiplication Cards (copy in blue)

Plus, or Positive, Cards (copy in green)

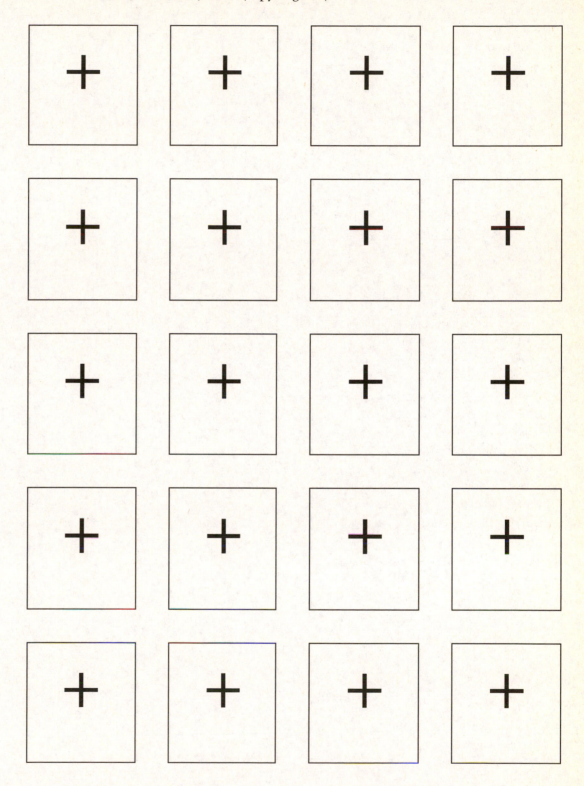

Negative, or Minus, Cards (copy in red)

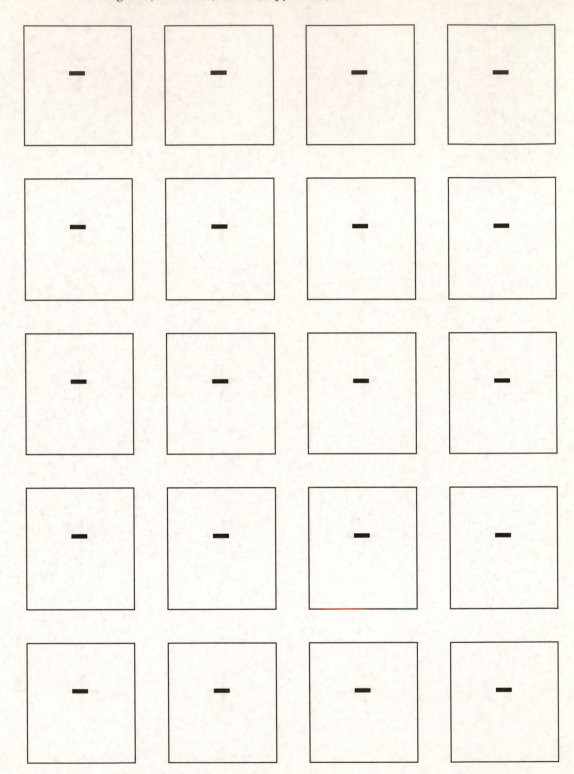

Variable Card X (copy in yellow)

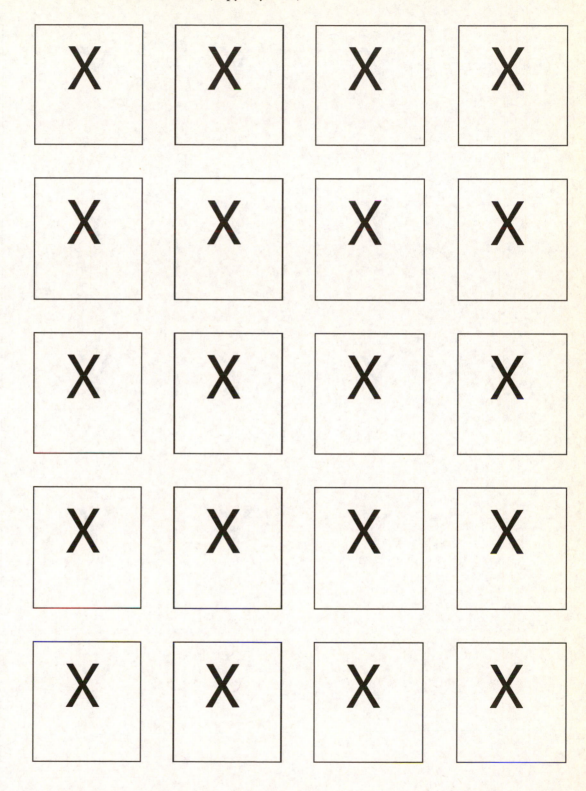

Variable Card Y (copy in yellow)

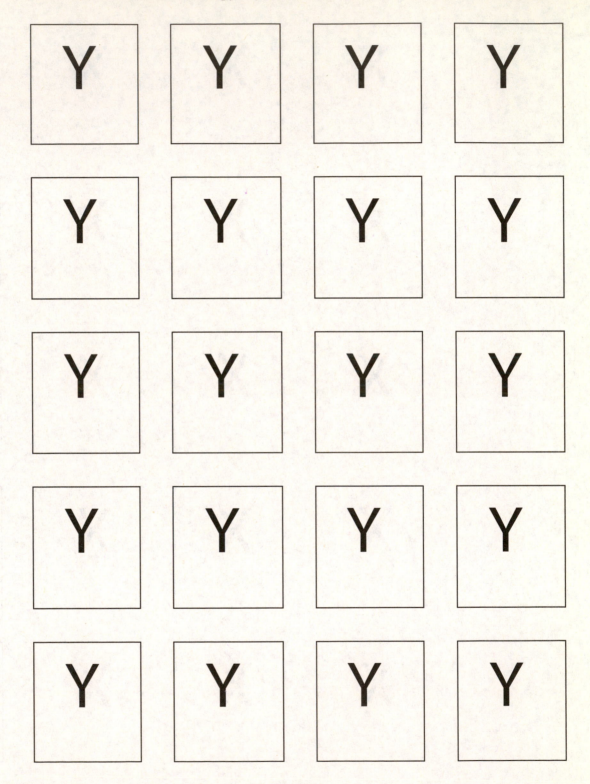

Variable Card Y (copy in yellow)

Variable Card N (copy in yellow)

N	N	N	N
N	N	N	N
N	N	N	N
N	N	N	N
N	N	N	N

Divisor Lines (copy in white)